Byzantine Armies

325 AD – 1453 AD

Byzantine Armies

325 AD – 1453 AD

DIMITRIS BELEZOS
M.A. in History

Illustrated by
CHRISTOS GIANNOPOULOS

AUTHOR
Dimitris Belezos

EDITORS (ENGLISH EDITION)
Nikos Giannopoulos, *Historian*
Stelios Demiras

TRANSLATOR
Thanos Mentzelopoulos

PROOF EDITOR
Charles Davis

COVER ART
Christos Giannopoulos

UNIFORM RESEARCH AND RECONSTRUCTION
Christos Giannopoulos

ART DIRECTOR AND COVER DESIGN
Thomas Nousias

MAPS
Thomas Nousias

First published in Greece in 2009
by Periscopio Publications
in cooperation with Squadron/Signal Publications

Distributed worldwide exclusively
by Squadron/Signal Publications
1115 Crowley Drive
Carrollton, TX 75006-1312 U.S.A.
www.SquadronSignalPublications.com

© 2009 Periscopio Publications

ISBN: 978-0-89747-577-8

DIMITRIS BELEZOS

Dimitris Belezos was born in Athens in 1975. He studied history at the History and Archaeology Department of the University of Athens and has an M.A. in Modern Greek History. He has written various articles related to the ancient and medieval world for the Greek magazines concerned with general and military history, published by Periscopio Publications. Five of his monographs, entitled *Crusades, The Latin Domination Era in Greece, Alcibiades, The Byzantine Army,* and *Knights*, have also been published in the Greek language by the same publishing company.

CHRISTOS GIANNOPOULOS

Christos Giannopoulos, an illustrator and figure designer, was born in 1968 in Athens. Although he has a degree and professional experience in Social Work, he has developed a special interest in ancient and medieval history. Christos has worked for 14 years as a professional artist and has produced illustrations for many children's titles, multimedia projects, and a number of books on ancient, medieval, and modern warfare. With his unlimited interest in figure design and uniform research, Christos has created original illustrations that have been a source of inspiration for a number of miniature sculptors producing figures for model companies, including Romeo Models and Pegaso Models of Italy, and Seil Models of Korea. His favored fields of study and research are Ancient Greek hoplite warfare, Celtic Europe, Central Asian cultures, and Roman Britain.

TRANSLATOR'S NOTES

What follows is a historical essay about the late Roman-Byzantine armies that protected the Byzantine Empire for over eleven centuries. It contains numerous military terms concerning the administration, ranks, logistics, weapons, campaigns, and fortifications of the Byzantine armies from 325 AD until the fall of the empire in 1461 AD. The majority of the terms are cited in the Greek language of that era, with the equivalent words in English and, where appropriate, Latin beside them in parentheses, i.e., *spathion* ("longsword"). Terms not in English are printed in italics in the text. At the end of the essay, there are glossaries of Greek and Latin terms to assist the reader in research and to help convey to a far greater degree, not only the military terms in the text, but also the extreme environmental conditions under which the Byzantine armies were forced to carry out their mission.

A NOTE ON TRANSLITERATIONS

All technical terms, titles, and most of the names cited in the text have been transliterated directly from their original Greek forms with as few changes as possible. Some names for which a standard English form is already very familiar, however, are written in that standard English equivalent form, such as Constantine instead of Konstantinos, John instead of Ioannis, and Thessalonica instead of Thessaloniki.

Contents

Introduction

The Byzantine State was considered by its inhabitants and administrators to be the natural continuation of the Roman Empire. From the 4th century AD, Roman emperors turned their attention to the Eastern provinces of the state and it was here that Constantine the Great founded a new capital, Constantinople, which marked the start of the progressive transformation of the Roman Empire into the Byzantine one. A few decades after the founding of Constantinople, the Roman state was split in two parts, the Eastern and Western Roman Empires. The Western Roman Empire finally collapsed in 476 AD under the pressure of the Germanic tribes and its former provinces lost all the basic principles of Roman mentality and tradition. However, the Eastern Roman Empire managed to survive for a further eleven centuries. Even if it progressively abandoned the Latin language for the Greek one, it maintained, to a large extent, the traditions of the late Roman Empire. Regardless of how much it altered externally in the centuries that followed, substantially its roots remained in the late Roman era. That said, the Eastern Roman Empire was, however, initially treated with animosity and scorn in western European historiography. The result of this negative attitude was the utilization of the term "Byzantium" in order to stress its difference from the ancient Roman state. The eleven centuries of Byzantine history were considered synonymous with progressive decline, court intrigues, and downgrading of all productive forces of culture, in a spirit of sterile bigotry.

Later, though, this negative perception changed and the Byzantine state was viewed in a somewhat more positive light. First came recognition of the centuries of protection Byzantium had offered to Western Europe. If the Byzantine Empire had not stood between the aggressive Eastern Mediterranean Muslims and the West, which had fragmented into small feudal states, perhaps the western Christian world would have collapsed long before the Renaissance era transformed Europe. In reality, however, the Byzantine Empire did not simply exist as the bulwark of western civilization. For centuries, the Byzantine state was western Christian civilization itself. For an extended period, during which the remains of Roman culture had disappeared from Western Europe, the Byzantine Empire served as the ark for the preservation of ancient Greek culture, the Christian faith, and the ideals of the Roman state.

These three elements, Greek culture, Christian faith, and Roman ideals, were unbreakably entwined within the idiosyncrasies of the Byzantines. They spoke Greek and their education was based on the study of the Greek classics. They considered the defense and dissemination of the Christian faith as their state's primary mission, realized through the cultural infiltration of neighboring peoples. During the entire life span of the empire, the Byzantines called themselves *Romaioi* ("Romans") and believed that they were the only legitimate successors and heirs of the Roman Empire.

This Byzantine attitude is revealed in many aspects of the imperial governmental organization as well as in the daily life of its citizens. The Byzantine army constitutes the most characteristic example. This in-depth presentation of its development reveals the checkered historical course of the empire, which was compelled to defend its territories and culture against a horde of belligerent enemies. There was no period of time during which the Byzantine state did not face the scheming of some neighboring tribe or state. During its long life span, the empire faced Persians, Goths, Huns, Lombards, Slavs, Avars, Arabs, Bulgarians, Russians, Hungarians, Normans, Crusader armies and, finally, the Turks. The survival of the empire proved to be a continuous struggle, the success of which resulted from its leaders' making the most of the courage, ingenuity, flexibility – and also the cruelty of the troops under their command. In consequence, the soldiers of the Byzantine Empire deserve recognition for, at least, a part of the splendor of the state they protected.

*CLIBANARIUS **OR CATAPHRACT MOUNTED LANCER** (970 AD - 1071 AD)*
The Byzantine Clibanarii or Klibanophoroi, as described in Nikephoros Phokas' Praecepta Militaria,
wore heavy armor made of different materials in successive layers: the first protective layer over the clothes
was zava - a padded cotton garment that prevented body sweat from rusting the outer layers of metal armor.
Next, came the lorikion – basic chain mail suit of armor that afforded protection to the upper body. The third layer of
defence was the klibanion of lamellar construction. Finally, over the klibanion, the lancers wore the epilorikion,
a thick padded garment made of waxed cotton that prevented the metal armor from overheating in the sun (it should be
noted that the word klibanion derives from the ancient Greek term klibanos, meaning "oven"). Other characteristic
features of this particular armor were the mail coif that completely covered the head, leaving only the eyes visible, the
lamellar shoulder and thigh guards, the segmented protection for the lower arms and knees and, finally, the toyfia
(painted horse hair tufts), that hung from the lancers' shoulders, first described in Leon VI's Taktika. Ian Heath, who
undertook the primary research on this uniform (published in 1979), suggested that, during this time, the Clibanarii
lancers would also have worn chain mail gloves. The horses were also well protected and carried heavy lamellar armor
(of polished metal or ox leather) and chamfrons. (uniform reconstruction and illustration by Christos Giannopoulos,
based on Ian Heath's and Angus MacBride's published conclusions and research)

The Romano - Byzantine army during later antiquity (325 AD – 642 AD)

The evolution and armed conflicts of the Empire

Diocletian's reforms

During the first half of the 4th century AD, the organization of the Roman Empire underwent important changes as a result of an extended period of internal realignments. From the era of Octavian, i.e. from the close of the 1st century AD, the Roman republic became a monarchy. In accordance with the Octavian reforms, the emperor shared power with the senate, the Roman aristocracy's supreme council. The emperor's role in this division of power was mainly military, as the holder of the imperial title controlled the provinces near the borders and, by extension, the Roman army, stationed there as a protective measure, was under his control. The only other military force, beside the border troops, was a unit of the Praetorian Guard quartered in Rome that served as the emperor's personal bodyguard. Members of this guard were selected from among the best legionaries of the military units along the borders.

Since the 1st century AD, the initial equal distribution of power between the emperor and the senate had already begun to shift in favor of the former. Succeeding emperors, exploiting their ability to control the Roman army, easily imposed their will on the senate that continued to exist in name only, being devoid of any real political power. Alongside the declining old democratic institutions, Rome was also

Armed conflict between Romans and barbarians. The legionary uses his sword (gladius) to attack the enemy and his shield to protect himself. Detail from a sarcophagus. (Rome, Araldo de Luca)

undermined as the empire's capital. The majority of the emperors were not from Rome but from the provinces. Many of them spent long periods of their reign far from the capital: on extended travels inspecting the empire, as did Hadrian (117 AD – 138 AD), or, like Marcus Aurelius (161 AD – 180 AD), on campaign. Rome finally ceased to be the pre-eminent city of the empire during Diocletian's reign (284 AD – 305 AD), when the empire was divided into four regions in order to ensure a more efficient administration. According to the Diocletian system, imperial power was shared between two Augusts (Emperors) and two Caesars. Each one exercised absolute political and military power within the region assigned to him, while the four collaborated on issues pertaining to the joint administration of the empire. When one of the Augusts died or resigned, the corresponding Caesar replaced him, after first appointing a new Caesar in the provinces he had administered until then. In this four-way division, Rome was not selected as the seat of any of the Augusts or Caesars, while Diocletian preferred to administer the Eastern provinces, even if he was the most powerful of the Augusts and Caesars, while entrusting the administration of Italy and Rome to others. It was this act by Diocletian that marked the shift of influence within the Roman Empire from the West to the East. Simultaneously, Diocletian also promoted changes in the empire's military organization. He stripped the provincial military governors of the political power they had wielded until then and confined them to strictly military duties. The number of troops was increased, but their training was limited, with the result that the Roman army acquired a reputation for indiscipline and unreliability.

Roman soldiers with a barbarian prisoner of war. (National Museum, Rome)

Constantine the Great's army defeats the enemy forces at the Milvian Bridge. (Painting by the School of Raphael, Vatican)

The Roman East, where Diocletian decided to reside, had a number of characteristic differences from the empire's western provinces. While Latin dominated in the West, in the East most of the inhabitants spoke Greek. In the Eastern provinces several important civilisations had blossomed in the past, including the Egyptian, the Phoenician, and the Persian; all, however, had over time been united under the most dominant civilisation of the Eastern Mediterranean, the Hellenic. Greek culture and language had prevailed in the East following the dominance of Alexander the Great and his successors from the end the 4th century AD. The East also constituted the center of trade of the Roman Empire. Important economic centers flourished, such as Alexandria, Antioch, and Thessalonica, cities that had also sprouted the actions of Alexander and his successors. The Eastern provinces also had one additional characteristic that proved to be of decisive significance for the historical course of the empire. This element was the Christian religion. Christianity had arisen in the East and was still more widespread there, in the early 4th century AD, than in the West. By shifting the weight of imperial power from West to East for the first time, Diocletian increased the weight of Hellenism and Christianity as far as the future of the Roman Empire was concerned.

The founding of Constantinople

The final shift to the East, and the intellectual and economic forces that dominated it, was overseen by Constantine the Great (306 AD – 337 AD), who suspended the quadripartite division of the empire and united the Roman state once again under a single authority. After concentrating power in his person in 324 AD, Constantine sought a new capital for the whole empire. He excluded the option of returning to Rome, whose geography was not considered suitable for commercial development. He also rejected the four capitals (Nikomedia, Nyssa, Milan, Treviri) that had been used during the period of Diocletian's tetrarchy and opted instead to create a new economic and political center. The site selected by Constantine for this purpose was in the region where the city of Byzantium already existed. The site of an ancient Greek colony, founded by the settler Byzas in 651 BC, the city had been destroyed by the Roman emperor Septimius Severus (193 AD – 211 AD) at the beginning of his reign and then later rebuilt by him in 196 AD. While it was a small provincial city, it was however situated on a most propitious site for the conduct of both seaborne and overland trade. Byzantium was situated at the easternmost point of the Balkans, where the Strait of Bosporus separated Europe from Asia and linked the Mediterranean with the Black Sea. It was the point where all commercial routes from East and West converged. As Byzas had done centuries earlier, Constantine understood the geographic importance of the city and decided to put it on the map.

In 324 AD, the implementation of an intensive building program began in Byzantium. The layout of the new city was completed in just six years and its official opening took place on 11 May 330 AD. The rapid progress of the works as well as the vast sums of money allocated for the realization of his vision are indicative of Constantine's determination for the development of a new administrative and economic center. According to the designs approved by Constantine, a city four times the size of old Byzantium was created and given the impressive name of "New Rome" *(Nova Roma)*. The new city encompassed an impressive palace for the emperor's court, while the old hippodrome was completely remodeled in order to serve the needs of a much larger audience. A building for senate meetings was also constructed, along with an extensive forum that, in Roman cities, corresponded to the function of the Greek *agora*, constituting, that is, the place where all economic and political activity took place.

Relief showing the two Augusti (Emperors) of the Diocletian period in military dress.

In order for the new city to be properly established, a number of poignant symbolic steps were taken: an arch, called *Milion*, was set up in New Rome that was to be used as the starting point for calculating distances between the empire's cities. Until then, this landmark had been situated in the center of Rome, where all roads traversing the Empire terminated. To underline the status of Constantine's city as the empire's capital, this landmark was now repositioned. This symbolic act clearly demonstrated to the empire's subjects that the seat of power of the Roman state had shifted to the East. Helen, Constantine's mother, placed parts of the True Cross on the arch of *Milion*, thus underlining the particular importance that the Christian religion had begun to attain throughout the empire.

Over the ages, successive Roman emperors had founded many cities, taking great care to adorn them with grand buildings. However, for the first time, an emperor had called a newly-built city by the name of the Roman state's former capital and then transferred to it state functions holding distinguished symbolic importance, such as a part of the senate. It remains unknown if Constantine had finally decided to transfer the capital to the new city that he himself had founded, and if he wished this new city to be named after him. During his reign, New Rome constituted the emperor's seat for an important period of time; however, the emperor also occasionally transferred his court to other cities. Finally, the new city became widely known, not by the name of New Rome, but as Constantinople, in honor of its founder. Perhaps this name prevailed after Constantine's death. It is, however, conceivable that this powerful emperor wished to connect the magnificent city he had designed and built with his name from the very beginning. It is also unknown to what degree Constantine understood the importance of founding a new city for the historical course of both the Roman Empire and humanity in general.

The predominance of Christianity

Apart from the final transfer of the capital, Constantine's name must also be connected with one more important change in the course of the Roman state, the predominance of the Christian religion. Constantine's shift from idolatry to Christianity was not realized instantly, but rather progressively and must be considered as the result of political expediency rather than sincere religious conviction. An explicit movement in favor of the Christians was the publication of the Edict of Milan in 313 AD while Constantine still shared power with Licinius (312 AD – 324 AD). According to the provisions of this decree, religious freedom was instituted throughout the empire. The right of absolute religious freedom was thus granted to the Christians, who had suffered merciless persecution or, in the best scenario, the distrust of the Roman state and the majority of its citizens. By this decree, Christianity was not imposed as the empire's official religion– this being impossible at that time, as the vast majority of the Roman populace were idolaters who looked upon the new religion with feelings of either animosity or indifference. Idolaters also dominated the army, a fact of which Constantine was very well aware. As he owed his hold on the throne to the faith of his army, he was not willing to risk the support that it provided him. Moreover, the emperor never ceased to adhere to, and respect the formalities of the old Roman religion and throughout his life he maintained the office of the archpriest (*pontifex maximus*) of the ancient gods.

A marble bust of Diocletian. He initiated a number of far-reaching military reforms, which were continued by Constantine. (Archaeological Museum, Smyrna)

Following the death of Constantine, the empire faced an internal crisis as his sons battled over the throne. After a protracted series of conflicts, the throne eventually passed to Constantine's nephew, Julian (361 AD – 363 AD), who earned the distinctive *Apostate* due to his last ditch effort to restore Roman religion to its former eminence, but also with important military successes against the empire's emerging opponents, the Germanic tribes and the Persians. Julian's expeditions along the Rhine and in northern Mesopotamia reveal the extent of the threat faced by the Roman state in the East and the West. Julian was killed in 363 AD during a retreat following a defeat in a battle against the Persians, although his followers attributed his death to assassination by the Christians. Whatever the cause, his death was the starting point for the final transcendence of Christianity. The emperors succeeding Julian formally maintained the office of the archpriest of the Roman religion until 379 AD, but nothing would prove capable of impeding the supremacy of the new

religion. Christianity combined better with the authoritarian regime that the emperors from the time of Constantine and afterwards wished to impose, because it supported the premise that the sovereign of the Roman state was God's representative on earth and was only answerable to God for his actions. Thus, the foundations for the formation of an authoritarian regime were in place, in which the connection of secular power with the Christian Church was a vital ingredient. Through a series of changes, the pagan Roman Empire was transformed into the Christian Byzantine Empire. The progressive predominance of Christianity, however, created a new problem in the Roman Empire, i.e. the birth of various sects among the Christians. These sects gradually developed into an important factor of destabilization of the state, with serious consequences for its internal stability and, in consequence, its external security.

The imperial division and barbarian raids

Christianity achieved absolute supremacy during the reign of Theodosius the Great (379 AD – 395 AD), who imposed Christianity as the official state religion and prohibited many Greco-Roman ceremonies, including the Olympic Games, held until then in Olympia, in southern Greece, to honor the god Jupiter.

The division of the empire into eastern and western departments accompanied the death of Theodosius in 395 AD. The western part included the Latin-speaking provinces with Mediolanum (current Milan) in northern Italy as its political center. The Eastern part included the Greek and other Balkan provinces, Asia Minor, the Asiatic provinces, that is to say, Syria and Palestine, and finally, Egypt and Cyrenaica (current east Libya) in Africa. The capital of the Eastern department remained Constantinople, which had increased in size and population and was fortified by a new, more substantial wall that was the most important, integral fortification structure until the Middle Ages. While the Latin tradition prevailed in the West, the Eastern provinces were characterized by the dominance of the Greek language and the Hellenistic culture, which had been established and flourished following the conquests of Alexander the Great. With this division, Hellenism in fact gained its own empire that it could vigorously develop.

The division of the empire coincided with the appearance of barbarian intruders along its European frontiers. Pressured by the Huns during the 4th century, several Germanic tribes began to move westward, seeking refuge in the Roman territories. Initially, the Roman Empire accepted them, hoping to utilize them as mercenaries. Soon, however, these refugees proved to be a destabilizing factor. In 378 AD, the Visigoths, who a few years earlier had fled to the empire's northern Balkan provinces as fugitives from the fury of the Huns, confronted the Roman army at Adrianople. In this battle, the Roman army was defeated and Emperor Valens (364 AD – 378 AD) was killed. Despite this, succeeding emperors continued to accept Germanic tribesmen in the imperial territories, granting them important privileges in return for their military services. These tribesmen, however, did not consider themselves as belonging to the imperial army, but formed their own units with their own chieftains as commanders. In return for their services, they usually received money or areas of Roman provinces in which they created their own semi-autonomous mini-states.

Although it suffered severe depredations from raids by the Germanic tribes, the eastern Roman Empire finally managed to halt their permanent settlement

(Opposite page) Members of the Emperor's Praetorian Guard. The guard was eventually disbanded, due to the excessive power it wielded, and replaced by the Scholae Palatinae.

on its lands. On the other hand, in the western Roman state, extensive territories were under the control of the Germanic intruders, having typically and substantially been divested of any Roman authority. The Franks had created a number of Germanic kingdoms in northern Gaul, the Visigoths were doing the same in southern Gaul and the Iberian Peninsula, and the Vandals established themselves in Carthage and a large swathe of North Africa. Roman sovereignty in the West was initially limited to Italy and the Mediterranean coasts of southern Gaul, while the capital of the western empire was transferred to Ravenna, a city on the northern coast of the Adriatic, which was protected from barbarian raiding by the marshes surrounding it. Finally, on 4 September 476 AD, the Germanic mercenaries deposed Romulus Augustus, the last emperor of the western Roman state, and seized power in Italy. At the same time, they recognized the formal suzerainty of the emperor of the East. In this way, the emperor of Constantinople became the only holder of the Roman imperial title again. However, in essence, Roman authority in the West had long been in decline and Roman culture had been seriously undermined. The Roman Empire was, thereafter, restricted to the Greek-speaking Eastern provinces.

Justinian's wars (527 AD – 565 AD)

The most significant emperor of the Eastern Roman Empire in the first period of its history was Justinian (527 AD – 565 AD). He had the rare ability of selecting the appropriate person for every high office. For his military adventures, he placed his trust in Belisarius, who enjoyed significant successes, primarily in North Africa and Italy. During Justinian's reign, the military might of the Eastern Roman Empire was restored, and the state did not need nor was immediately threatened by foreign mercenaries. This re-vitalization proved, to a certain extent, the salvation for the empire because, during that period, the Byzantine army was forced to fight on many fronts. In the East, the empire suffered from Persian aggression while, in the West, Justinian engaged his state in extended campaigns with the goal of regaining the western Roman provinces. When Justinian assumed power in 527 AD, the Eastern Roman Empire had already been at war with the Persians for almost a year. This war continued until an agreement of "Eternal Peace" was achieved in 532 AD, allowing Justinian to attempt the reduction of the Vandal state in North Africa a year later. The Vandals were subjugated within a short period of a few months; this, however, did not bring about the final pacification in the newly established province of Carthage, as the kingdom was named after its capture. In 536 AD – 537 AD, a military mutiny in the territory sparked a number of battles with Mauritanian natives living along the fringes of the desert, beyond the province's borders. Clashes with the Mauritanians continued until 539 AD, then resumed in 543 AD, and ended with the final victory of the imperial army in 548 AD. From then on, peace prevailed apart from some minor skirmishes in 563 AD. Italy, however, remained the region where Justinian's interests and the majority of his military efforts were concentrated. The struggle against the Ostrogoths, the Germanic tribe that controlled Italy, commenced in 535 AD and continued until 552 AD with the final subjugation of this powerful Germanic people by General Narses, Belisarius having been dismissed under a cloud of suspicion. The war in Italy, however, was not over. From 553 AD to 554 AD, the region

(Opposite page)
A Roman emperor accepts the unconditional surrender of barbarian warriors.

Construction of a fortress on the borders of the Roman Empire. (Detail from Trajan's Column, Rome)

suffered a number of raids by the Franks and the Alamanni, while at the same time the Imperial army completed the occupation of the north of Italy, and established the line of the frontier of the new province along the Alps. Justinian's western conquests were completed in a comparatively short period, from 552 AD to 555 AD, with the occupation of part of Andalusia in southern Spain. The empire, however, was unable to muster sufficient forces in order to continue the campaign against the Visigoths who dominated the remainder of the Iberian Peninsula.

While Justinian's military successes in the West were impressive, the security of the Eastern provinces, which were much more important, was neglected. Repossessing Rome and Italy was, in essence, simply a question of prestige, devoid of any essential value. Asia Minor and Syria, on the other hand, actually constituted the economic heart of the empire, and these lands found themselves in mortal danger from Persian aggression. Khosrau I, the Persian king, took advantage of the emperor's lack of interest in the Eastern borders and attacked without warning. This caused the Imperial army immense problems, as it was forced to fight a protracted war on two fronts until 561 AD. In addition to the Italian and Eastern frontier wars, the Eastern Roman Empire faced yet another threat: the barbarian tribes living north of the Danube were constantly threatening to invade the northern Balkan provinces. The presence of these barbarians, although less powerful than the Italian Ostrogoths and more disorganized than the Persians, threatened the very existence of Constantinople itself and its vital territory. According to Justinian's political opponents, however, this state of affairs was not caused by the inefficiency of the army, but rather by the weakening of the frontier guards due to the transfer of too many troops to the West. They also accused him of tolerating the barbarian raids in the hope that, by doing so, he would convince their leaders to fight as mercenaries during the campaigns for the re-occupation of Italy.

In the West, the largest area subjected to Justinian's reconquests and for which the empire had undergone considerable sacrifices, success proved to be somewhat short-lived. In 568 AD, almost three years after Justinian's death, the Lombard, another Germanic people, appeared along the northern borders of Italy. Many of them had served as mercenaries in Narses' army some years before and knew the region. The Lombards managed to infiltrate into the Italian provinces and seize a large swathe of the Italian countryside from Imperial control. Soon, the newly arrived intruders held sway over the majority of the Po valley and Tuscany. Roman power had been confined to a number of important, well-fortified cities, including Ravenna, the Western Roman Empire's former imperial capital. Outside the walls of these major cities, however, the empire's sovereignty was, at best, somewhat tenuous. The Lombards constituted a permanent threat to Rome itself, the seat of the Pope who was patriarch of all the regions that formerly belonged to the Western Roman Empire. The Lombards also expanded into southern Italy, although there they faced stiffer resistance. Roman sovereignty actually remained firm in the regions of Calabria and Sicily, where the vast majority of the population was Greek-speaking, as well as the islands of Sardinia and Corsica. Imperial control over southern Iberia was also progressively lost. Subsequent to these developments, Italy, after its repossession, instead of becoming a rich province capable of considerable contribution to the economic blossoming of the empire, remained a constant source of problems and a factor that drew the Emperor's attention away from the emerging Persian threat in the east. To ensure their best defense, the western provinces were split into two large administrative areas, called *exarchates* governed by an *Exarch*. The first exarchate included the Italian provinces with Ravenna as the capital, while the second, covering the North African provinces of the western Mediterranean, had Carthage as its capital.

Justinian was also forced to confront an internal problem of the empire, the continuously increasing influence of powerful large landowners. These had begun to assume too much power, becoming one more faction challenging central authority. Some of them owned fortified manors and private armies, and were always attempting to extend their estates by pressuring the yeomen to give up their land in their favor. These large landowners were a major threat to imperial power, and Justinian was forced to take punitive measures to curb their power.

The Period of Heraclius (610 AD – 641 AD)

The power of the Persians grew more threatening during the reign of Phocas (602 AD – 610 AD), as they occupied northern Mesopotamia and Central Asia Minor, reaching the Asiatic coast of the Bosporus directly opposite Constantinople.

The Exarch of Carthage, Heraclius, took advantage of the discontent of Constantinople's population over these developments and sent his fleet, commanded by his son, also named Heraclius, to claim the imperial throne. In 610 AD, the son overthrew Phocas with little difficulty. During the first years of his reign, however, he failed to vindicate the aspirations of the people of Constantinople, who had initially regarded him as the empire's savior. In fact, for some considerable time he undertook no initiatives against the empire's enemies who, meanwhile, had flagrantly occupied vitally important territories. The Persians eventually took possession of Asia Minor in its entirety, apart from the northern and western coasts. King Khosrau II also occupied Syria and Egypt, as well as Palestine. The economic and moral consequences of this march of events were inestimable. The empire's granaries were deprived of Egyptian grain, while Alexandria and Antioch, the East's two important financial centers, ended up under Persian control. Jerusalem and the rest of Palestine, a region of particular religious significance for the Christian Roman Empire, given that Jesus had lived and taught there, were also occupied. Indeed, the Persians provocatively carried off the Holy Cross of Jesus, the holiest of Christian relics, to their capital, Ctesiphon, as loot. The barbarian tribes living north of the Danube, the Avars being the most powerful among them, took advantage of the opportunities offered and joined forces with the Persians, invading and occupying the majority of the northern Balkans. Only the southern part of the Hellenic peninsula and a few fortified cities, including Thessalonica, remained under the empire's control. Constantinople found itself under constant threat, with the Avars carrying out raids outside the city walls and the Persians having settled on the opposing Asiatic coast. With this crisis facing the Eastern Empire, the Italian Lombards saw their opportunity to exert yet more pressure on the remnants of Roman power in the region.

By 620 AD, the empire's situation was dire. As far as territories were concerned, it had shrunk to small areas of the Greek coastline, Asia Minor, parts of Italy, the large islands of the Mediterranean (Sicily, Sardinia, Corsica, Crete and Cyprus) and the Exarchate of Carthage. Emperor Heraclius viewed the future of his state with pessimism and set about working out a plan to transfer the capital to Carthage. He attempted to justify this idea to his advisers, maintaining that, in North Africa, the only region of the empire that was not threatened by outside forces, he could reorganize the imperial army and then return later and recover what had been lost. The senate, dominated by the Patriarch Sergius, explicitly refused to endorse his plan. Indeed, it was pointed

Battle formation, known as the "turtle," used during sieges of cities and forts. Detail from Trajan's Column. (Rome, Araldo de Luca)

out that Heraclius, as Emperor, was obliged to defend his capital and not retreat before the barbarian threat. Under this pressure, Heraclius was compelled to take action and, in 622 AD, he launched a campaign against the Persians in Asia. His aim was not only to recover the Roman provinces annexed by the Persians, but also to strike at the heart of the Persian Empire itself in central Mesopotamia.

After five years of continuous conflict, the Persians were finally defeated at the Battle of Nineveh in 627 AD. A conspiracy then broke out against King Khosrau II, forcing him to eventually conclude peace terms with the Roman Empire that specified the return of all the territories occupied by the Persians during previous expeditions. Heraclius had been victorious, rescuing the empire from a direct danger. In addition, he had recovered all the lost territories, as well as the holy relics seized by the Persians from Jerusalem.

The Church, which had contributed a portion of its wealth for the conduct of the war, also constituted another basic factor of the victory. The triumph led to the final formation of the Empire's political ideology and its citizens' perception regarding their state's position in the world. According to this perception, the Roman Empire was a state protected by God, the safety of which constituted one of the primary concerns of the divine force. Jesus and the Virgin Mary supported the defense of the empire and, particularly, its capital along with its defenders. The Emperor was Christ's representative on earth and was considered equal to the Apostles, and should henceforth be portrayed with a halo like the Saints of the Church. Thus, the Roman Emperor, the deified archpriest since the time of idolatry, became revered as a saint equal to the Apostles following the predominance of Christianity. In this way, his special position was clearly maintained between his subjects and the supernatural world. In addition, of specific importance was the position of the Church and, in particular, the Patriarch of Constantinople, who was designated as one of the most important personages of the empire. However, this development elicited a fierce reaction from the Pope, who claimed for himself primacy among the leaders of the Christian world.

After Heraclius' victory over the Persians, the idle passiveness that had, until 622 AD, characterized the initial period of his reign once again prevailed. Meanwhile, with everything indicating that the Persian threat had been neutralized, the empire found itself once more confronted by a much more powerful and dangerous opponent, the Muslim Arabs. The populations of the Arabian Peninsula, which up to this time had been culturally backward and politically unorganized, were united under the leadership of Muhammad, a former merchant, who had risen to prominence as a preacher of the new religion of Islam. Following Muhammad's death in 632 AD, the Arabs sallied forth against both the Persian and Roman Empires, intending to spread their new religion at swordpoint. By 642 AD, a year after Heraclius' death, the Arabs had totally subjugated the Persian state and had seized Syria, Palestine and Egypt from the Roman Empire. Antioch and Alexandria had, once again, been lost, as well as Jerusalem with its priceless religious relics that were to be found there. This march of events also altered the character of the Roman Empire. Confined in the ensuing centuries to the Greek-speaking regions of Greece, Asia Minor, and southern Italy, the empire would be forced to confront mortal danger on a permanent basis.

The remains of Hadrian's Wall, which protected Roman England against raids by the northern (current Scotland) barbarian tribes.

The organization of the army of Constantine and his successors

The Roman frontier line *(Limes)*

The empire that the Roman army was to protect during Constantine's reign extended from England to Mesopotamia, entirely covering North Africa and the Mediterranean coastline. The northern frontiers of this vast state extended to the banks of the Rhine and Danube rivers, although Roman power also covered the region of Dacia (current Romania), on the northern bank of the Danube. The southern borders extended to the northern fringes of the Sahara desert, which meant that the empire was in no danger of attack from that area, as the desert constituted an impassable obstacle for any prospective invader. In the east, the empire shared a common border with the Persian state. Part of the border was common with the fringes of the Arabian Desert, while to the north-east, the Asian frontiers of the Roman state extended to northern Mesopotamia and the Caucasus. This region was a bone of contention between the Romans and Persians.

The bulk of the Roman army was usually encamped close to the borders ready to protect them. These encampments were located at regular distances from each other and small settlements usually grew up around them that, in certain cases, developed into important cities. In those provinces situated far from the borders, only a few legionaries were stationed, their basic mission being the maintenance of order and supporting the tax collection. The only military unit to be found in Rome until Constantine was the formerly elite Praetorian Guard whose primary mission was the emperor's protection and which was finally disbanded by Constantine himself.

The Romans considered the borders sacred and believed that any violation of them should be harshly punished. Of particular concern were the northern frontiers, along the Rhine and the Danube, where barbarian races constantly mounted raids on Roman territory. In these regions, a state of continous war or military readiness to confront the direct threat of invasion prevailed for long periods of time. The inhabitants of the Mediterranean basin did not immediately conceive the seriousness of the situation prevailing in the north, as the barbarian raids were intercepted at the frontiers. During the mid-3rd century, however, Germanic tribes managed to infiltrate into and along the Mediterranean coasts causing severe depredation in Greece and even sacking Athens. The situation along the Eastern borders was less complex, because here the Roman army was confronted by the well-ordered Persian Empire and not by disorganized barbarians. While its army was more organized than the Germanic hordes, the Persians did not hesitate to attack powerful fortresses or even cities along the Eastern borders, often with considerable success.

In those regions where the Roman frontiers were difficult to define, the frontier legions often delimitated them by constructing distinctive landmarks, such as a road or, in a number of cases, regular walls, often extending for many kilometers. These structures actually constituted a Roman-style miniature of the Great Wall of China. The most famous of these walls separated Roman Britain (modern northern England and Wales) from the barbarian inhabitants from the north of the island (modern Scotland), with a number of points of this impressive fortification structure surviving even today. These strongholds were manned by legions, a force that numbered approximately 5,000 men in its early form and 1,000 men in the Late Imperial era. Each legion was an autonomous military unit, capable of moving independently, as it comprised units of infantry, cavalry, engineers, and the necessary logistics personnel.

According to law, a legionary had to be a Roman citizen. This pre-condition lost its importance, to a certain extent, from 212 AD, when Emperor Caracalla (211 AD – 217 AD) granted Roman citizenship to all the empire's subject populations. Slaves and barbarian mercenaries from regions outside the Roman state were still not permitted in the legions, but the Roman army did use them in separate units, usually composed of fighters from a single tribe or region (*foederati*). These auxiliary units were assembled into three categories, the "Wings" (*alae*), composed exclusively of cavalry, units of infantrymen (*cohortes peditae*), manned exclusively by foot soldiers, and units of horsemen (*cohortes equitae*) that were, inexplicably, manned by a combination of horsemen and infantry. These auxiliary units numbered 500 (*quingenaria*) or 1,000 men (*milliaria*). During periods of emergency, such as the preparation of a campaign or the interception of a surprise invasion, the Roman army could proceed with the recruitment of barbarian mercenaries en masse. In this case, the organization of these irregular auxiliary units was not so strict.

The Roman state's defensive structure was partially altered by Marcus Aurelius (161 AD – 180 AD). He created military units organized as reserves to support areas of the frontier that faced the most clear and eminent danger. These new units were able to move more easily compared with the frontier army and they were also available to take part in expeditions. Their legionaries were trained for a more

The two Augusti (Emperors) and the two Caesares from Diocletian's time. The four leaders of the Roman Empire appear in military dress. (This relief was later removed to decorate the front portal of St. Mark's Cathedral in Venice)

*Roman soldiers
at the beginning
of the 4th century AD.*

aggressive, versatile method of war as opposed to the frontier soldiers' primary mission that was the defense of strongholds and passes. Marcus Aurelius also brought about one more important change; he abrogated the criterion of an officer's social origin as a prerequisite for promotion and established, as an exclusive qualification, the candidate's ability to attain an administrative position. This change strengthened the emperor's position against the already undermined senate because, until then, the majority of military governors were selected exclusively from among members of the senators' families. The next change in the empire's military organization must be attributed to Septimius Severus (193 AD – 211 AD), who increased the legionaries' salary. By so doing, he tried to improve the security of the Imperial frontiers, while also ensuring his hold on power, as the Roman army controlled the path to the Imperial throne.

Constantine's reforms

Constantine the Great completed the process of reorganizing the Roman army that Marcus Aurelius had started. From the time of Constantinople's founding, the Roman army had been divided into three types of unit. The frontier guardians, also called *Ripenses* from the Latin term *ripa* meaning bank, were maintained as a military unit. This name was given to them because banks of rivers demarcated quite a large part of the borderline. During the 4th century, they were also called *Limitanei*, from the term *limes*, as the Romans called the frontier line. The *Comitatenses* units, organized to participate in campaigns and pitched battles, were more flexible. The *Comitatenses* received their title from the term *comitatus* meaning "the emperor's entourage," and they were so named as they always remained under the emperor's direct command. There was also the emperor's guard, the *Scholae (Scholae Palatinae)*, whose troops were called *Scholarioi*. This new guard replaced the Praetorians as the latter had meddled excessively in the political life of the empire and had attempted to control the process of imperial succession. The units of *Scholae Palatinae* were under the Emperor's direct command, unlike the Praetorian unit that was commanded, on the Emperor's behalf, by another senior officer. For the unit's administration and

*(Opposite page)
Colossal bust
of Constantine
the Great. By founding
Constantinople
and offering protection
to the persecuted
Christians, Constantine
cleared the way
for the transition
from the Roman
to the Byzantine era.*

A Roman emperor addresses his soldiers. (Detail from Constantine's Arch, Rome)

economic management the Scholae depended on the *Magister Officiorum*, who clearly had a political role but had no hand in its military mission. The precise organization of the *Scholae* during Constantine's reign is still unknown. Later, however, the troops serving in them were divided into units of 500 men, each unit under the command of a *tribunus*.

The Comitatenses army was separated into infantry and cavalry units. The commander-in-chief of all infantry units was the *Magister Peditum* ("commanding officer of the foot soldiers"), while the *Magister Equitum* ("commanding officer of the horsemen") commanded the cavalry units. Of equal rank was the *Praefectus Praetorio* ("custodian of the praetorium"), who was the commanding officer of the Praetorian Guard. Following Constantine's military reforms, however, the duty of the *Praefectus Praetorio* was to be in charge of the army's catering and logistics.

The *Scholae* were excluded from jurisdiction over the two military leaders, as the latter were answerable directly to the Emperor. The *Magister Peditum*, in common with the *Magister Equitum* held the high command of the *Ripenses* and *Comitatenses* armies. The division of the armed forces' high command between two equivalent government officials was, since the days of the republic, quite usual in Roman political and military administration as a means to prevent the concentration of power in one person. As the title *Magister* was also awarded to other military dignitaries, the *Magister Peditum*, or *Equitum*, was also given the title *Magister in Praesenti* or *Magister Praesentalis*, meaning commanding officer in the Emperor's presence. This was to add emphasis to the fact that his place was at the Court under the Emperor's direct supervision.

The *Comitatenses* army was not located at just one point in the empire, but was rather spread across a number of provinces. The most important *Comitatenses* units were stationed in Gaul, Illyria (modern north-western Balkans), Thrace (this province included the entire north-eastern part of the Balkans), and the Eastern borders. Each of these units operated under the overall command of a *Magister* or *Magister Militum*. The full title afforded these officers included the region he oversaw, that is *Magister Militum per Gallias* for Gaul, *Magister Militum per Illyricum* for Illyria, *Magister Militum per Thracias* for Thrace and *Magister Militum per Orientem* for the Eastern borders. Each *Magister* had his own staff (that, in Latin, was described by the term *officium*), consisting of the *Officiales*. The number of staff officers varied, depending on the Magister's situation and the extent of the territory over which he commanded. For example, historical reference reveals that, in 441 AD, a *Magister Militum* had 300 *Officiales* at his disposal.

This organization of the Eastern Roman Empire resulted in the separation of high military power, as different *Magistri Militum*, *Peditum* and *Equitum* held joint administration. This change favored the central imperial power, which could not now be threatened by an ambitious general. There was thus

established in the East the notion that the emperor held sole overall command of the army, regardless of whether he had held an army command or had any previous military experience. All the other military dignitaries held part of the High Command but never its grand total. In the Western Roman Empire, however, the opposite organization prevailed and, in the final decades before its demise, the *Magister Peditum Praesentalis* continued to hold overall command of the entire army in the West.

In addition to the *Comitatenses* units, there were also other military units in the provinces that did not directly guard the borders, but constituted the first *Ripenses* reserves. These troops were also called *Comitatenses* but were paid a lower salary. In fact, the regular *Comitatenses*, in order to underline their precedence, were also called *Palatini*, thereby adding emphasis to the fact that they constituted the Emperor's real army and were not simple frontier guards. The *Ripenses* units were divided into legions, cavalry and other auxiliary units. During Constantine's reign, the legions did not remain stationed in large encampments as happened previously, but were dispersed in small outposts along the borders. In each legion's central encampment there could be a force of 1,000 - 1,500 legionaries, with the remainder divided into smaller units of 500 troops. These regulations applied to infantry units, to which the engineer units remained attached. The mission and organization of the cavalry were changed accordingly. The legion's heavy cavalry became an independent unit so that it could cooperate better with the light cavalry of the auxiliary units, which were divided into *Cuneos Equitum* and *Auxilia*. Until quite recently, very little was known about the *Cunei Equitum*. In Latin, *cuneus* means "wedge," consequently the name of these units can be translated as "cavalry wedge." This term is possibly in reference to their formation in battle inspired by Alexander's

Representation of part of Diocletian's palace at Spalaton in Croatia (modern Split). That palace was designed using frontier encampments as a model. (Mostra Augustea, Rome)

Constantine the Great addresses his soldiers before the start of the battle at the Milvian Bridge.

Companion cavalry which used similar (originally Thracian) tactics to penetrate into enemy lines. *Auxilia* constituted the successors of the older *Alae*, that were units of light auxiliary cavalry.

During periods of peace, the troops remained in their encampments. The *Ripenses'* camps were positioned along the borders and, in some cases, were isolated even if, as mentioned earlier, settlements (invariably small) usually sprang up round the larger frontier fortresses. By contrast, the headquarters of the *Comitatenses* forces were always situated in big cities. The empire's frontier line consisted of a complex system of fortresses, outposts, and supply stations. In the case of an invading force managing to overcome the first line of defense of the *Ripenses*, they would then be confronted by the second line of fortresses, while powerful units of *Comitatenses* were found in all of the empire's big cities (the primary objective of any invader). The protective network along the borders was augmented by an equally well-organized system of direct, rapid dissemination of intelligence from all units to the central administration, so that the transfer of reinforcements could be effectively coordinated and the Roman governors would be aware of every movement of the enemy.

The basic training of the soldiers was considered to be of particular importance. The recruits initially passed a trial period *(probatio)* before being accepted in their unit. The usual age of recruitment was between 20 and 25 years, but later, the lack of troops stretched the age limits from 18 to 35. For legionaries, there was a minimum height limit, initially 5.1 Roman feet (1.77 meters – 5.75 feet). Later, once again due to the emergencies and a marked lack of civilian interest to serve in the legions, this limit was reduced to 5.07 Roman feet (1.70 meters). According to the regulations, the officers in charge of recruitment had to check the recruits' physique and general health. The basic criteria for someone to be considered capable of serving in the army were sparkling eyes, straightness of the neck, a broad chest, the appearance of the muscles of the arms, shoulders, legs and the rest of the body, particularly in the stomach area. Legionary recruits should also have long fingers (probably to be able to throw a spear straighter and farther).

Recruiters also had to check the social and professional origin of the recruits. Slaves, and anyone whose profession was considered humble, including fishermen, tannery workers, cooks and householders or employees of inns and taverns, were excluded. Butchers, hunters, construction workers and blacksmiths, however, were considered suitable to serve in the army. The inhabitants of rural areas were considered more suitable for military service than men from the cities. According to Roman army beliefs, recruits originating from the provinces were used to hard work and hardships of all kinds while, by contrast, those coming from the cities were characterized by a propensity for luxury and indulgence.

The selected recruits spent at least a four-month period of hard training, during which their physical and mental endurance was put to the test. After completing basic training, the new legionary was tattooed with the military symbol or, instead of the tattoo, received a small lead disk *(signaculum)* that hung around his neck, took the military oath *(sacramentum)*, and was officially included on his unit's list. According to the military rituals, the oath was taken in two phases. A legionary first read the entire text of the oath and then the reqruits, one after the other, repeated the phrase *idem in me* ("the same applies to me"), while holding their sword to their necks. This gesture symbolized their determination to sacrifice themselves for the emperor and the acceptance of the hard punishment that awaited anyone who broke his oath. Only after this procedure could the recruit be included in his unit records and be officially considered a soldier. The soldiers of the empire were separated into infantrymen *(pedites)* and cavalrymen *(equites)*. A soldier's military rank depended on the total years in service, but the individual's military ability and bravery were always taken into consideration. (For the recruitment and initial training of the legionaries see *The Late Roman Army* by Pat Southern and Karen D. Dixon, London, 2000, pp. 73-75).

A bust of Constantine the Great cast in copper. (National Museum, Beograd)

Officers of the Romano-Byzantine army

The administration of the *Ripenses* was a task of the *Duces* (*Dux* in singular). The term in Latin means "person in command" or "leader" – the word "duke" is also derived from this. Initially, in the Roman army, an officer who occasionally held command of a larger number of military units either to transfer them or to conduct a campaign held this title. By the 3rd century, however, the title *Dux* had already been included in the regular hierarchy of the army. Each of the *Duces'* assumed authority in one or more provinces. Nevertheless, contrary to the older Roman practice in place since Diocletian's time, the military provincial governors no longer undertook any kind of political administration; rather, this was undertaken by a *Praeses* (Latin for "guardian" or "protector") in each province. Consequently, each *Dux* was only in command of the military units of the *ripenses* that were stationed in the provinces he administered, and not for the general supervision of the political administration in these regions.

The full title of the *Duces* was supplemented by the name of the region that each administered i.e. the *Dux Africae* was the person in charge of the Roman provinces of north-western Africa, while *Dux Aegypti* was the same in Egypt. In other cases, if they administered more than one province along the frontiers, they were simply called *Dux Limitis* in order to emphasize the fact that their mission was safekeeping the *limes*, the Roman borders. A general geographical determinant concerning the provinces they had under their administration could also be added to this title, as was the case with the *Dux Limitis Scythiae*, the title of the person in charge of the northeastern borders. The *Duces'* area of responsibility, however, was not always clearly defined, but varied depending on the needs of each period and the magnitude of the threat faced by each region. The *Duces* were also called *Comites* (*Comes* in singular) or *Comites Limitis*. Initially, this term meant "attendant" or "companion," while later it characterized a dignitary with a certain commissioned service of administrative, economic or military nature. The Comites with military responsibilities were called Comites Rei Militaris and their duty occasionally extended from the administration of some insignificant frontier post to monitoring entire provinces. The title was usually identified with the office of the *Dux*, however. Besides the *Magistri Officium*, staff (*officium*), consisting of *Officiales*, surrounded the *Duces*.

Helmet originating from the area of the Danube. (The Museum of Vojvodina, Novi Sad, Serbia)

The *Duces* came under the authority of the *Magistri Militum*, even if they reported directly to the emperor in certain cases. Their basic mission was to protect the regions they administered from hostile invasions. For this purpose, they were charged with the discipline as well as the training of the troops under their command, and saw to the maintenance of fortresses within their jurisdiction. The maintenance of fortifications of any kind was particularly important, as the basic mission of the *Ripenses*, which were commanded by the *Duces*, was the defense of fortified positions, as opposed to the *Comitatenses*, that were trained for open field battles and, generally, for mobile war. Another basic mission undertaken by the *Duces* was also the recruitment of new troops to man the units under their command. Constantine insisted that all *Duces* should personally inspect the recruits and select those suitable for military service. The *Duces* also checked their troops' food supplies. For this, they reported to the *Praefecti Praetorio* ("custodians of the praetorium"), who were the persons in charge of the army's economic

The emperor takes part in a ceremony following a victory. (Detail from Constantine's Arch, Rome)

management. The *Duces* were also responsible for the application of military justice and acted as judge for those soldiers who had fallen foul of military law. Formally, they belonged to the class of horsemen, the second in importance in the Roman social hierarchy after that of senator. Emperor Valentinian I (364 AD – 375 AD), however, promoted holders of the rank, declaring that they should also belong to the same class as that of senator, as well as the remainder of the superior dignitaries.

The army's lower ranking officers were called *Praepositi*, *Tribuni* or *Praefecti*. The term *praepositus* was not initially part of the official hierarchy, but denoted the commanding officer of a military unit, usually consisting of auxiliary troops or mercenaries but not legionaries, but over time it was applied differently. Later, the title was attributed to commanding officers of smaller units permanently stationed at some point of the empire. Depending on the units in which they served they were distinguished as *Praepositi Scholae*, if they belonged to the emperor's bodyguard, *Praepositi Legionis*, when they belonged to some legion, or *Praepositi Cohortis*, if they were in command of a smaller unit of legionaries. There was also *Praepositi Equitum* for the cavalry and *Praepositi Auxilii* for the auxiliary units of barbarian mercenaries, whereas the general term *Praepositi Militum* was also used in some cases. The *Praepositi* played a very significant role in the organization of the *Ripenses*. The regions of the borders that were under the jurisdiction of the *Duces Limitis* were divided in smaller ones, each one under the authority of a *Praepositus Limitis*.

The military ranks of lower officer ranks that were current in the days of the Roman republic remained in use, but new designations were added to them in the later period. The highest rank was that of *Primicerius* followed by that of *Senator*, whose duties are still unknown. Concerning *Senator*, we are only aware that it was an infantry unit rank and was in use within legion infantry units and the *scholae*. A lower rank than that of *Senator* was that of *Ducenarius*, commanding officer of a small unit of 200 men. This rank was used for the *scholae* and also for units of infantry and cavalry. The basic junior ranks were those of *Centurion* (*centurio* in old Latin. Since Constantine's time, however, this rank was also awarded the title *Centenarius*) and of the *Decurion* (*decurio*). Other under officers included the *Biarchus* (a term of Greek origin) and the *Draconarius*. A *Biarchus* was, to all intents and purposes, the quartermaster, while a *Draconarius* was of equal rank and his duty was to carry the unit's military emblem, which often took the form of a dragon *(draco)*. In addition, two *Numerarii*, who dealt with economic affairs usually served in each unit.

Catering for the Romano-Byzantine army

A Western Roman Empire emperor in military dress. (Barletta, Italy)

The existence and dispersion of such a large army was bound to create critical problems as far as its administration was concerned. Although the catering of the army was quite a complex operation, it was, nevertheless, achieved smoothly, due, above all, to the well-oiled bureaucracy within the Roman Empire. (Eventually, the neglect of logistics could be considered the beginning of the decline of the Roman army and the final collapse of the Roman state and culture in the West). The collection of foodstuffs for the soldiers *(annona)* and forage for the army's livestock *(capitus)* usually took place three times a year. The quantities thus assembled were then stored in government-owned fortified depots *(horrea)* and guarded by the army. However, the persons in charge of counting and distributing the food supplies were not military, but political appointees. These depots were often found in, or near the *Ripenses* camps, the troops of which were also responsible for their security. In some cases, the supply of foodstuff for the *Comitatenses* took place in a somewhat less organized manner, as these units were often on the move or in transit. If a *Comitatenses* unit was stationed in a region where there was no government-owned military depot, a portion of the province's inhabitants' tax contributions could be used for the unit's provisioning.

The distribution of supplies was always done under strict supervision and each transport and delivery was minutely recorded. The persons in charge had to calculate and maintain a daily record of each portion of food that was distributed. Unit commanding officers, specifically the *Duces*, were responsible for updating the persons responsible for the catering in regard to the actual muster number of each military unit, so that waste and corruption could be avoided. Quite a few of the camps along the borders, however, produced part of their essential supplies in cultivatable areas close by or purchased supplies from the local market. In some cases, this practice was also encouraged by the central administration's habit of not sending supplies to the units but, instead, forwarding pecuniary sums for purchasing the necessary supplies. In the Western Roman Empire, this practice progressively prevailed while the logistics services were neglected. Instead of foodstuffs, the soldiers received only a pecuniary sum as an addition to their salary with which they had to supply themselves with everything necessary for their survival. In the Eastern Roman Empire, meanwhile, military logistics continued to function regularly and the provision of money replaced the distribution of supplies only in special cases.

The Roman legionary's diet was well organized. It consisted mainly of bread, fresh and salted meat, mainly pork, wine, and oil. The inhabitants of the provinces supplied the cereals, oil, and wine through the imposition of taxes. The wine offered to the legions was produced in the region in which they were stationed and, in some cases, it could be replaced with beer, specifically in the northern provinces of Europe. The bread was provided by local guilds of bakers or landowners. The basic diet was supplemented with quantities of cheese, fruit, vegetables, dried fruit, poultry and eggs, fish and other kinds of seafood, especially oysters. On roving expeditions away from the camps, provisioning was different. During the long campaign marches, the legionaries received rations of hardtack (*bucella* or *bucellatum*), bread, wine, vinegar, salted pork and beef, and they were trained to carry up to 20 kilos of supplies. Food consumption was organized in three-day cycles. During these cycles, the legionaries consumed the fresh bread on the first day, and the *bucellatum* during the next two. The consumption of hardtack remained with the Roman and Byzantine armies for centuries. The Byzantines later called it *paximadion* or *paximation* (from where the modern Greek word for "rusk" originates). They also ate salted pork for one day and beef for the other two, while every two days they alternated between wine and vinegar. During the campaigning season, it was the inhabitants, without exception, of the particular province where the army was operating who were obliged to bake the army's bread and hardtack. Sometimes, the grain intended for bread could be used in the preparation of a tasteless soup, which was particularly detested by the troops.

Similar regulations were also in place for the supply of forage for the horses and also for any other livestock. The *Ripenses'* units usually had their own pastureland for their animals. The *Comitatenses* units, as well as other units frequently on the move, had to use other pastures, often against the wishes of the inhabitants of those regions. With the decline of the Western Roman Empire, the troops behaved arrogantly towards the populations they were supposed to be protecting and, generally, took what they required. In the Eastern Roman Empire, however, provisioning of the army continued in the same well organized, controlled, disciplined manner. That said, it was incumbent on the citizens of the empire to offer hospitality to the soldiers when they were on the march. In these cases, the troops were accommodated in private residences or inns. Weapon manufacturers, painters, priests, doctors, and schoolteachers and, in certain cases, workshop owners were exempt from this obligation, however. According to regulations, the second best third of the residence accommodating a guest soldier *(hospes)* was reserved for him, the householder retaining the remaining two thirds of the residence for himself and his family. The guest soldier could only request shelter and nothing more. This regulation was often violated, however, with the soldiers forcing the householder to provide food and to wait on them.

The legionary's arms

Apart from food and fodder, the Roman army also supplied its troops with their clothing. The legionary's basic uniform included a top (in Latin *sticharium*), a tunic (*chlamys* in Greek-Latin), a cloak *(pallium),* and military footwear. It is not known how often these items were replaced, but the provision of clothing and footwear was progressively replaced by grants of money, as with the provisions mentioned earlier. The distribution of weaponry and horses was handled in a similar way, although information about these items is scarce. While on campaign, the Romans did not hesitate to use looted materiel, provided that these arms were equal to the Roman ones and the soldiers had been trained to use them properly. In all other cases, the captured materiel that was deemed unusable was destroyed.

It is difficult to provide an accurate description of the Roman legions' weaponry during the time of Constantine and his successors, because the uniformity that had earlier prevailed in the Roman army was gradually abandoned. This was due to the progressive admission of barbarian mercenaries and the adoption of some items of their weaponry. The operation of state-run industries *(fabricae)* producing items of weaponry did, however, ensure a modicum of uniformity, at least in regular army units. The legionary's offensive weapons were a long sword *(spatha)*, in some instances a dagger *(pugio)*, and the classic spear of the Roman army *(pilum)*, although new spear types had already begun to appear. The most important of these was the *hasta plumbata* or simply *plumbata*, which was actually the precursor to the *martzobarboulon* used by the Byzantine armies in the succeeding centuries. Spears of this type were separated into two categories, *hasta plumbata et tribolata* and *hasta plumbata mamillata*. The former were cylindrical and had a metal or wooden grip ending in a metal point. The grip had small feathers attached to its bottom end in order to steady the spear in flight. The *plumbata mamillata* had a lead weight behind the point and feathers at the opposite end of the grip. Each soldier carried five *hastae plumbatae* in the recess of his shield. These weapons could be used both offensively and defensively, though the precise method of their use is unknown. In some instances, Roman soldiers also used broadaxes, while there were also separate, specialized units of archers *(sagitarii)*.

The legionaries' defensive armament consisted of a helmet, a breastplate and a shield. The helmet was of metal, usually consisting of a part that covered the top of the head down below the nape of the neck and two movable cheek guards. The rear of the helmet, which covered the neck, was squared off. The cheek guards protected quite a large area, often leaving just the eyes uncovered. A decorative peak was fixed to the top or, in some cases, the forehead of the helmet. The breastplates were made of interlocking metal rings *(lorica hamata)* or small steel plates *(lorica squamata)*, connected by leather or linen strips. The shields were usually oval, about 1.1 meters high and up to one meter wide. On the outer side was painted a representation of the unit's symbol as well as the bearer's name and century.

The majority of the Roman army's weapons were produced in the government owned industries of weaponry production (*fabricae*, singular *fabrica*), although usually, only regular units were equipped by the state; the recruited mercenary units provisionally providing their own weapons. These state industries were generally situated in important cities. By doing so, they could take advantage of the existing infrastructure, including other local industries that provide support, auxiliary material, suitable lodgings, and food for the workers. More important, they provided security for the produced weapons, to prevent them falling into the wrong hands. During the 4th century, twenty such *fabricae* functioned in the Western Roman Empire with a further fifteen or so in the east. The most common *fabricae* were those that manufactured shields and other types of basic weaponry (*fabricae scutariae et armorum*) and these were situated throughout the empire.

Yet it was in the east that the empire's enemies made more use of their bows in battle, thus forcing the Romans to counter this with numerous archers. It is, however, likely that local industry production covered the army's requirements in this area, which made the existence of large government owned industries unnecessary. In the Eastern Roman Empire, meanwhile, there were three industries that produced weapons for the heavily armed horsemen, because troops of this type were used only against the Persians. This is contrary to the Western Roman Empire, where the use of heavily armed cavalry was somewhat more infrequent, and where only one industry existed for the manufacture of corresponding weaponry; although this was not independent, but was part of a wider *fabrica armorum*. Diocletian also created industries for the manufacture of military clothing, a practice that also continued throughout Constantine's reign.

The legionaries' payroll

In addition to their food and clothing, the legionaries also received some kind of a salary (*stipendium*). The basic salary was the *annona*, which was identified as the minimum salary that each soldier deserved. The officers, on the other hand, were awarded much higher salaries, depending on their rank. Senior officers were paid up to five times that of the lowest ranked soldier's basic *annona*. Those serving in the cavalry received an additional amount (*capitus*) for the maintenance of their horses. Contrary to what happened with the *annona*, both soldiers and officers received the same amount as *capitus* and only some senior officers could receive more (which was twice as much). This salary was progressively increased in order to also cover their needs for food, clothing, and weapons, especially when these were no longer provided by the state – it nevertheless constituted an important part of the Roman soldier's income. The salary was disbursed three times a year. Cavalrymen and certain select foot soldiers received 600 denarii annually, while the rest of the legionaries received 400. Those serving in the auxiliary units received 200 denarii annually. These amounts remained unchanged for centuries, which, as a result of inflation, diminished their purchasing power. To counteract this, the soldiers' salary was supplemented by donations proffered by the emperors on certain occasions, such as the anniversary of their birthday or their ascent to the throne. The amount received by a legionary in this way was called *donativum* and, the regular disbursement of such sums constituted a respectable additional salary. During Diocletian's reign, each legionary received 1,250 denarii for each August's anniversary and roughly about half that amount for the Caesars' feasts. Thus, the annual income of a legionary could amount to around 7,500 dinars.

Those serving in auxiliary units were similarly remunerated. To be more specific, each soldier in those units received 250 denarii for the Augusts' feasts, resulting in an annual income of about 1,250 denarii. The officer's salary was larger. At the beginning of the 4th century, a *Praepositus* would receive 18,000 denarii as *stipendium*, increasing to around 54,000 after the addition of various donations. Later in the same century, the *stipendium* was increased up to 36,000 denarii, but the actual market value of the salary was not significantly altered because of inflation. The officers, however, could legally retain a part of the provisioning allowance of the unit they commanded. This practice allowed them to boost their income considerably, but the practice was open to abuse by many officers, especially in the remote frontier garrisons.

Special gifts were distributed on the occasion of an emperor's ascent to the throne. At the assumption of the imperial title, Julian (361 AD – 363 AD) gave each legionary 5 gold coins *(solidi)* and a quantity of silver, equal in amount to 4 gold *solidi*. The exact amount depended on each emperor, but it was considered a regular and long-established practice. In addition to their regular income, soldiers would also receive a number of unscheduled rewards as an extra incentive for better performance in battle. During his campaign against the Persians, Julian promised 100 silver coins to each legionary who distinguished himself by his bravery. Additional incentives could be offered to soldiers for their loyalty during a military coup for the overthrow or to show support for an emperor. In these cases, the party that prevailed awarded those troops that supported it with generous rewards. The regular payment of salary and the gifts constituted an important factor for the maintenance of discipline. If the troops remained unpaid for a long period of time, it was likely that they would become indisciplined or even desert to the enemy. (The facts mentioned above can be found in *The Late Roman Army* by Pat Southern and Karen. D. Dixon, London, pp. 77-78).

The legionaries' personal life and retirement

In the pre-Constantinian Roman army, any soldier or officer lower in rank than centurion had no right to marry. During Constantine's reign, this restriction was lifted, and the soldiers' families were allowed to live together with them in the camps. This regulation caused a severe logistical problem for the military organization, because the question was then raised with regard to whether the state also had to supply provisions for the members of the soldiers' families. Until 372 AD, the state did, in fact, provide food for their families. In that year, however, Emperor Valentinian I (364 AD – 375 AD) issued a decree stating that the soldiers would have to provide provisions for their children themselves. It should be remembered that the soldiers' families constituted an important source of recruits, because the soldiers' sons were compelled to follow in their fathers' profession. The soldiers also deserved a leave of absence, on condition that a senior officer, usually a *Dux*, *Magister Militum,* or *Comes Rei Militaris*, granted it. In fact, it was common practice for both junior and senior officers to grant soldiers leaves of absence from their units by levying various amounts of money. This practice was illegal, however, and if the transaction were discovered, the officer

Illustration of a fortified Roman mansion.

responsible would be punished with property confiscation or, in the case that hostilities broke out during the soldier's absence, the officer could face execution.

A soldier could retire after a long service career, usually 24 years. Those who successfully completed their military service were granted an *emerita missio* ("meritorious discharge"). A military service career could also come to an end after 20 years but, in this case, the soldier was granted the *honesta missio* ("honorable discharge") instead, and was also granted fewer privileges than those who had served the additional four years. Many soldiers, however, chose to remain in the army as long as they could in order to continue receiving a regular salary as well as the additional rewards, although this practice caused problems with the promotion of junior officers. If a soldier was forced to abandon military service due to wounds or health problems, he was granted the so-called *causaria missio* ("justifiable discharge"), which corresponded to *emerita* or *honesta missio* under certain conditions. Any member of the *Comitatenses* was granted *emerita missio* whenever he was unable continue in the army because of wounds or other health problems incurred during his service.

On the other hand, the *Ripenses* were only granted *honesta missio* if they had completed 16 years service and their inability to continue serving was only due to wounds received in battle.

The released soldiers were given the relative certificate and, by making use of it, they were able to claim veterans' privileges. They were also granted exemption from the *capitatio*, which was a kind of poll tax. Those who had been released after 20 years service or with a *causaria missio* were also granted equivalent privileges for their wives. In earlier times, those who had completed 24 years military service were also granted exemption from the *capitatio* for a further four individuals. Constantine limited this right, however, stating that those who had completed 24 years military service were granted exemption from the *capitatio* only for themselves and their wives. Veterans were also exempted from a number of other minor contributions, such as taxes for the market operation and transportation. As compensation, at the end of their military service veterans could receive either a monetary grant in order to start their own business or a parcel of land for farming. If they chose to cultivate the land, their service would also ensure them (in addition to the land) a pair of oxen, a small monetary grant and 100 *modii* (Roman measurement unit) of wheat. Emperor Valentinian I later revoked the monetary grant in these cases, but increased the provided quantity of grain, especially for the emperor's bodyguards. All other veterans would only receive 50 *modii* of grain. The land awarded to retired soldiers was usually in an area of not much interest to other farmers and consequently was not very fertile.

The army's decline and the barbarian mercenaries

The most important change in Constantine's military organization occurred under Theodosius the Great (or Theodosius I, 379 AD – 395 AD), who was responsible for admitting a large number of barbarian mercenaries into the Roman army. The majority of the empire's citizens, however, particularly the residents of Constantinople, were uneasy and, indeed, hostile to the Germans following the defeat and death of Emperor Valens at the hands of the Visigoths at the Battle of Adrianople in 378 AD. The Germans were permitted to settle in certain territories of the empire, often in the same regions they had previously plundered or threatened, and allowed to create their own semi-independent hegemonies that, to a large extent, were outside the control of the central Roman administration. The starting point for this march of events was the concession of a leave of settlement to the Goths in 382 AD.

Initially, this convention was presented as a continuation of the old Roman practice. For centuries, the Roman army had engaged the services of different barbarian tribes, but these mercenaries had never been given as many rights as in 382 AD. Until then, the practice followed by successive Roman administrations consisted of recruiting young, fierce warriors as mercenaries, a practice that, if they were allowed too much leeway, could constitute a significant danger to internal security. These warriors were either divided into small groups and then attached to units of the Roman army, or were drawn up as a new, autonomous Roman unit. In the latter case, however, the barbarian mercenaries had to undergo training by the Romans before entering military service and then they were transferred to a region far from their homeland so they would not constitute a destabilizing factor. In this way, the danger of fomenting revolt against the central authority was diminished. Theodosius, on the other hand, allowed the Germans to remain under the administration of their leaders and to settle in any territory they wished. Until that time, the mass recruitment of mercenaries under these terms was highly unusual in the Roman Empire and only occured in periods of crisis. Theodosius argued that this agreement was the best solution in order to protect the Balkans and Constantinople itself from the barbarian raids. His opponents, however, and also the barbarians with whom he had joined forces, viewed this decision as a weakness in the empire's ability to effectively defend its territories.

Indeed, the policy did reflect the inability of the regular Roman army to protect the empire. The circumstances that brought about the decline of the Roman army and, eventually, of the empire itself, due to the collapse of its defensive forces, are the subject of considerable historical debate in which various opinions have been put forward. It is certain, though, that during Theodosius' reign the size of the regular army was considerably reduced and its training gradually neglected. The army's cohesion was also loosened, with its units being deployed in numerous cities, since the barbarians threatened not only the frontiers, but also major areas of the vast territory of the Roman state. Each city and settlement, however small, had to be guarded. But breaking up the army into small garrisons in separate cities undermined the spirit of unity of the force and prevented the joint close-order drill of soldiers in large military formations. The precise number of troops under the orders of the Roman Empire remains unknown. During the reigns of Diocletian and Constantine, the Roman army numbered between 450,000 and 600,000 men. While this number may, perhaps, appear impressive, the extent of the frontiers that had to be guarded must be taken into consideration, as well as the fact that armies of that era required greater human resources as they did not have the firepower of a modern army. It is a fact, however, that following Julian's death, overall troop numbers began to decrease on a regular basis.

The barbarians sack a Roman city.

The 382 AD agreement caused the massive translocation of barbarian populations to the empire's interior, as new mercenaries came to settle in those regions that Theodosius had granted them and their families. Other barbarian tribes also requested and received similar terms. Indeed, some barbarians even attempted to press for terms with the Emperor after they had transgressed the empire's borders. The total number of those who crossed the frontiers and finally settled in Roman territories amounted to hundreds of thousands. The members of the mercenary units swept in by this flood tide of immigration were called *Foederati* from the term "foedus," as the agreement between them and the Emperor was called. The *Foederati* groups did not always emanate from the same tribe. In certain cases, they were simply barbarian adventurers who had joined together under the command of a common leader. Initially, according to the agreements with the *Foederati*, the Roman state would be responsible for their maintenance through the regular provision of supplies *(annona Foederatica)*. In this way, the provisioning of the mercenaries was dependent on the empire, which thus maintained some control over them. Progressively, however, this provisioning exercise changed to an annual payment of given sums of money that, in consequence, increased their autonomy.

The demand for mercenary services was so widespread that some barbarians also served other employers apart from the emperor. Thus were created the groups of *Bucellarii*, a term derived from the word *bucella* or *bucellatum*, meaning the Roman army's hardtack. They initially served powerful landowners, and defended the properties and mansions of their employers from the raids of other barbarians or rapacious gangs. Progressively, however, the term *Bucellarii* also included some of the mercenaries serving in the imperial army, specifically those that had been recruited following a private agreement with a general rather than with the imperial army.

The barbarian mercenaries evolved much differently in the Eastern than in the Western Roman Empire. Although, initially, the eastern part of the Roman state faced the invasion of more barbarians, it finally managed either to eliminate, or absorb them. By contrast, in the Western Roman Empire, the semi-independent settlements of barbarians finally developed into regular states that eventually led to the dissolution of the entire western empire. The *Foederati* also followed a parallel course. Disorganized mercenary units remained in the West, until the demise of Roman power in 476 AD. On the other hand, in the east they were progressively absorbed into the organization and discipline of the Roman army. From the 6th century onward, the *Foederati* constituted regular military units of the Eastern Roman Empire, trained and disciplined in the same way as the rest of the regular units. All undisciplined barbarians who were recruited under agreements and terms similar to the old *Foederati* were, henceforth, called by the Greek term *symmachoi* ("allies"). This process of eliminating the danger by absorbing the barbarians was not painless, however. The Goth general Gainas, for example, assembled such powerful forces in Constantinople that they eventually threatened the Eastern Roman Empire with barbarization. He was overthrown and the Goths slaughtered in Constantinople in 400 AD.

The level of power and influence exercised by the barbarians in the Roman army can be better understood when the large number of Germans who attained the senior rank of *Magister Militum* is taken into account. Prominent among them are the Vandal Stilicho, the Goth Frabitas, and the Franks Arbogast and Bautus. There were many more barbarians holding other, more junior ranks in the Roman military hierarchy. The most formidable of the German barbarian leaders was the Visigoth, Alaric I who, at the close of the 4th century AD, plundered Greece, perhaps with the tolerance of the imperial government that wished to destroy the cradle of the ancient, idolatrous religion. After Greece, Alaric turned his Visigoths towards Italy, where he plundered and destroyed Rome in 410 AD. Two years earlier, in 408 AD, some courtiers under the orders of the Emperor Honorius of the Western Roman Empire had slaughtered the Germans serving in the emperor's guard, without, however, achieving their aim of altering the situation. In 407 AD, the Roman legions withdrew from Britain, and then in 411 AD, from the Iberian Peninsula. The Western Roman Empire progressively shrank while its regular army went through an advanced stage of disintegration. Local city guards in the West collapsed following the arrival of the barbarians and the end of economic support from the central administration. By 476 AD, when the western Roman state officially ceased to exist, its army had long been dissolved.

Recruiting the Empire's citizenry

The disbandment of the army and the need to recruit barbarian mercenaries was due, to a large extent, to the lack of volunteers from the empire's interior. For the imperial army, a certain number of willing volunteers were always on hand, but the majority of the recruits were sourced through conscription. The Emperor Diocletian commanded that all sons of veterans be required to enlist in the Roman Army provided they were suitable for service. Constantine modified this rule, saying that the sons of soldiers could serve either in the army or in the local administrative service. Diocletian also imposed an annual conscription of men from the provinces. The number of recruits demanded was directly in proportion to the terms of the payment of taxes. Each landowner was to offer a number of men that worked on his properties in a proportional percentage to the taxes he paid. Only important public office holders were exempt from this contribution. Based on this regulation, the powerful landowners had to offer one or more recruits each year, while the rest contributed in turn. That is to say, each year a different landowner offered recruits and thus everyone's obligations were progressively covered. This recruitment, however, was often substituted by the payment of a special tax, called *aurem tironicum* ("deliverance gold").

The recruits, according to the law, had to be members of the landowners' families and not slaves. This clause was often violated, however, because the landowners did not want to send their children to join the army and, as a result, they would send slaves for military service. Indeed, landowners did not offer the recruiters strong, intelligent, capable men, because these were required for work in the estates. Thus, during the recruitment, individuals put forward for military service were often unfit for any useful purpose and the landowners just wanted to be rid of them. Another major problem was the high rate of desertions, especially among the young recruits. In certain cases, officers in charge of recruitment were forced to shackle the recruits each evening or lock them up in the local prison until their transfer to a camp for training was completed.

The Roman state tried to reverse this development in a number of ways. From 380 AD, several attempts to impose the mandatory recruitment of the sons of the old soldiers were made. Jail sentences were also imposed on those who offered slaves instead of free citizens for military service, as well as to those who tried to avoid conscription through self-injury causing minor physical disabilities. In 406 AD, however, despite recruiting barbarian mercenaries, the lack of troops in the Western Roman Empire was so severe that the recruitment of slaves was allowed without restrictions. These slaves were, moreover, promised their freedom on the expiry of their military service. The Roman army, however, did not simply require men; it needed well-trained, disciplined soldiers. The Roman Empire needed its citizens; these, however, trying merely to survive in a difficult era and being distrustful of the state that had, until then, failed to protect them from the barbarians' incursions had no interest in helping. Thus, undisciplined barbarians, who ignored the most basic elements of Roman civilization and the Roman administrative system, were called upon to fill the void that was created. Their recruitment, however, was about to have the most disastrous results.

Fortifications in the later Roman state

The fortresses, found mostly along the borders *(limes)*, were of particular importance for the organization of the Roman army and the defense of the empire's frontiers. During the first centuries of the Roman Empire (from the 1st to the end of the 3rd century AD) the Roman army preferred to confront the barbarian invaders in open battle rather than hiding behind the walls of fortresses. This was, of course, due to the Roman generals' confidence in their troops, whith training and discipline that gave them a massive advantage, especially in the west. The Eastern front was a different matter, as here they were confronted by the regular Persian army that was equal to the Roman one, at least as far as training and organization were concerned. Along the rest of the empire's frontier regions, however, the Romans were confronted by disorganized barbarian hordes, which they could crush, not only outside the legion's fortresses but, quite often, before they could infiltrate the empire's territories. Nevertheless, after the disastrous barbarian raids in the middle of the 3rd century, the legions were forced to revise their tactics and remain based in their fortresses to a far greater extent, considering them a refuge and a last line of defense if they were unable to overwhelm the invaders in regular, pitched battle. As the barbarian raids could increasingly reach the empire's interior, the fortifications also began to expand beyond the border regions, the camps or the frontier settlements, inside many cities, large country estates and monasteries across the empire's provinces, in some cases far from the frontiers.

A line of fortresses, constituting a continual line along the frontiers, protected the empire. During the 3rd century, the fortresses were strengthened by the construction of sturdy towers along their outer walls, especially at the corners, as well as by reducing their circumference to make them easier to defend. In certain fortresses, all the exterior gates, apart from one, were barred. The walls and the towers of most fortresses were reinforced in order to withstand the impacts of siege engines. In earlier times, the fortresses were built square, without taking into consideration the terrain on which they were situated but, by the 3rd century, this practice had also been abandoned and the walls began to be constructed to conform to the terrain. This fact proves that, henceforth, the legion fortresses ceased be looked upon simply as guarded camps and were progressively turned into bases in which the Roman army could seek refuge when the nearby countryside was occupied by barbarian invaders. In addition, the new fortresses were no longer built on level ground, as they had been in the old days, but rather on hilltops. This made them less accessible to an invader while giving the defenders an uninterrupted field of view of the adjacent territory. These fortresses were called *refugia*. A typical fortress of that era was the *quadriburgium* ("four-towered fortress"), which consisted of a square stockade with a tower at each corner. The design of a four-tower fortress acted as the basis on which Diocletian's palace at Spalaton in Dalmatia was also built. These fortresses acted as autonomous military bases that, apart from lodgings for the soldiers and their families, had their own weapons stores and food warehouses, a form of chapel, and stables for the unit's animals. Due to limited space, the *Principia* ("Headquarters") was rather small.

Front view of a helmet found in the Danube region. (The Museum of Vojvodina, Novi Sad, Serbia)

*The barbarians attack
a Roman city.*

Similar changes also took place across the transportation system. Until the
3rd century, Roman roads were completely safe; after that time, however,
security was increased with the construction of fortified towers and other control
points at specific points. Many bridges and other strategic crossroads were also
fortified. From early times, a number of *mansiones* ("buildings") had been built
along the Roman roads where dignitaries, soldiers, and postmen could stop
overnight during their journeys. Some of these were also fortified, while new
burgi ("fortified stations") were also constructed. The term *burgi* was used to
describe a line of fortifications that included fortified stations as well as smaller,
independent towers. Those towers were usually used as observation posts to give
early warning to the frontier troops of an imminent barbarian raid.

The fortification of cities was considered of vital importance. Up to the 3rd century, the walls of many cities had been neglected, primarily, because of the prevailing sense of complete security. Then, during the second half of the 3rd and the beginning of the 4th century, the walls of most cities were strengthened and, in addition, more towers were built. The fortification of the cities usually took place at the initiative of the local council, as the cities of the Roman Empire always enjoyed a relative internal autonomy. On the other hand, in the case of major cities that constituted military or administrative centers or held an armaments industry, the central administration contributed considerably to their fortification. So, because from that time onward, the interception of the barbarian invaders at the borders was no longer a certainty, the weight of the defense of the empire shifted from the frontier fortresses to the fortified urban centers.

The walls of Constantinople

The most noteworthy case of fortification of a city during that period of unrest was the construction of the walls of Constantinople. Constantine the Great, during the founding of the city, designed a wall that over the succeeding decades proved to be somewhat inadequate. A number of the Eastern Roman Empire's capital's outer districts extended outside these fortifications, particularly along the coasts. The creation of a new, extensive line of walls was, therefore, necessary. New walls were built between 405 AD and 423 AD, with construction beginning during Arcadius' reign (395 AD – 408 AD) and ending during Theodosius II's (408 AD – 450 AD) reign. These walls are, perhaps, the most impressive example of early medieval fortification architecture because of their strikingly massive construction. The triple walls were primarily constructed from stones and bricks and constituted three lines of defense. The first line of the defense of Constantinople consisted of a moat 7 meters (20 feet) deep and 20 meters (61 feet) wide (these, and the following measurements are approximate). The sides of the moat were made of walls 1.5 meters (5 feet) thick. The moat was vertically separated by sections of walls, the interior of which carried Constantinople's hidden aqueduct pipes. On the inward bank of the moat was a 2-meter (6-foot) high wall, further encumbering its crossing by any would-be intruders. After this first wall there was an open corridor 20 meters (61 feet) wide (called *parateichion*), before the first line of walls. These first walls were 0.8 - 2 meters (2 to 6 feet) thick and 9 meters (28 feet) high on the outer side. On the inner side they were lower, however, reaching just 3.5 meters (10 feet) high. On the inner side of the outer walls was another open corridor, the *peribolos*, 14 - 15 meters (50 to 65 feet) wide. After this, there was the second line of walls, with a thickness ranging from 5 meters (15 feet) at the base to 4 meters (around 13 feet) at the top and a height of 10 meters (30 feet) at ground level and 13 meters (40 feet) on the inner face, which faced the city center. The only point where the walls had a different configuration was on the northern part, where Blachernae's imperial palace was situated and, because of this, here the fortifications were even stronger.

The wall had ten primary gates and a number of smaller secondary entrances. Five of the ten gates had bridges crossing the moat constituting Constantinople's connecting points with the countryside. The five other gates

Section of the fortifications and walls of Constantinople.

were constructed for military purposes, in order to facilitate the movement of troops from one point to another. Each of the inner wall's gates was protected by two heavily constructed towers, which covered the largest part of the precinct at that point. In contrast, the outer wall's gates were simple arches, just slightly higher than the fortifications surrounding them. At regular intervals, towers strengthened both the outer and inner wall. The outer wall's towers were 10 - 12 meters (30 - 36 feet) high and protruded 5 meters (15 feet) from the wall. There were 96 towers along the inner wall; each 30 meters (90 feet) high and protruding 6 - 11 meters (18 – 33 feet). While these towers were incorporated in the wall, they were, however, constructed as separate buildings so that they could better withstand any attempt by an enemy to undermine them. The most impressive of all the gates was the one in the southern part of the walls that was called "Golden Gate." It was, initially, a triumphal arch, built as an independent structure in 390 AD and then later incorporated in the walls. Victorious emperors, following a successful campaign, always entered Constantinople through this gate.

Along the coast of Constantinople was constructed a sea wall, which, in the appearance and dimensions, corresponded to the city's outer walls. This sea wall, however, was not afforded the same level of attention as that of the inland wall, because, at the time of its construction, the empire held absolute control of the sea and any attack against the coasts of Constantinople was considered highly unlikely. To further ensure the security of the city, a long chain was extended along the Golden Horn gulf, on the north side of Constantinople, which prevented hostile ships from approaching from that direction. This chain was attached to two towers situated on the opposite coasts and supported on wooden rafts on the water. Each ring of the chain measured .66 meter (2 feet) in length.

The Byzantine army
from Justinian to Heraclius

Justinian's army

Justinian's army, although relatively small in numbers and characterized by frequent bouts of indiscipline by both officers and troops was, nonetheless, dignified by notable successes on a number of battlefields. The well-organized Persian military machine was successfully halted, although peace eventually prevailed because of certain diplomatic and economic concessions. The kingdom of the Vandals was subjugated in an incredibly short space of time, in a campaign reminiscent of the German "blitzkrieg" of the 20th century, while its neighboring African tribes were driven back beyond the borders of the empire, despite their ability to raise large number of warriors. The Ostrogoths, because of their power and doggedness, were, on the other hand, a more resolute opponent and prolonged their resistance beyond any anticipation, much to the surprise of Justinian's generals. Finally, however, they too were forced to yield. Even in the northern Balkans, regardless of the continual pressure and short-lived successes of the barbarian intruders, the imperial army finally secured the frontier along the Danube and forced all the invaders back from whence they had come without their having succeeded in settling in any of the empire's territories. Confronting so many opponents across vastly different geographical areas compelled the imperial army to apply a wide variety of battlefield tactics as well as methods of logistical organization.

The basic characteristic of the Byzantine army during this period was its versatility, in conjunction with its ability to both construct and capture fortresses. Justinian's engineers reduced all types of fortification that they confronted. Following the subjugation of a region, Byzantine dominance was completed by the construction of powerful fortresses, which were invulnerable to any barbarian attacks.

Another important characteristic of the time was the gradual predominance of the Greek language across all areas of the Eastern Roman Empire's administration. All the Latin military terms were progressively hellenized or replaced by equivalent Greek ones. Although Latin formally remained the empire's second official language and a large part of the military commands and terminology continued to be Latin or Romanic throughout the 6th century, in the end most were dropped, as the majority of the troops became Greek-speaking. Even the barbarian mercenary units, who, for the most part, were indifferent to what language was used, finally preferred the Greek language, as it was the language being spoken throughout the empire they served.

The units of the Byzantine army during Justinian's time

During the 6th century, the imperial army retained, to a large degree, the organization of the Roman army as it was during Constantine's time. The Eastern Roman Empire's military forces during Justinian's reign consisted of

regular units in which the empire's citizens served, and mercenary units, made up of barbarians. The regular units were divided, as in earlier times, into units of *Limitanei, Comitatenses,* and the Emperor's Guard. Units of the *Bucellarii,* comprising either barbarians or citizens of the empire, were also used. Groups of foreign mercenaries were, however, usually included in the units of the *Foederati.* Army divisions were further supplemented with units of the *Ballistarii,* which handled the *ballistae* ("stone-throwing catapults"), and the armed units used for the security of the cities or certain country regions.

The primary mission of the *Limitanei,* as earlier, was border protection. Because they safeguarded those remote fortresses, from then on they were also called *Milites Castellani* or *Castresiani,* in other words, "fortress troops." These units were made up of forces of infantry and cavalry. Justinian's conquest of new provinces led to the creation of new *Limitanei* units for the protection of the empire's extended borders. In Italy, a new *limes* ("border line") was created along the Alps. The troops serving in the *Limitanei* units had already changed since the 5th century and become soldier-farmers, who cultivated land granted them by the state in return for their services. The plots of land granted for this purpose were called *loca* or *territoria castellorum* ("places or regions of the castles") or agri *Limitanei.* By this time, however, the Limitanei units had already largely lost their military character and limited themselves to police-type duties connected to safeguarding the borders. This change led to a reduction in their salary and privileges, and thereafter they were not considered to be regular soldiers. The title of 'soldier' was henceforth attributed only to the *Comitatenses* and to those serving in the emperor's bodyguard. Following the peace agreement with the Persians in 532 AD, Justinian changed the location of the *Limitanei* units in the East, with corresponding negative impact on the standard of living of those serving in those units and downgrading of the empire's defense.

Justinian is represented in St. Vitellius of Ravenna as head of the imperial procession. To the right of the Emperor can be seen his bodyguards holding their weapons.

Illustration showing the proclamation of an emperor being crowned by the Patriarch while both stand on a shield. (Illustrated manuscript from John Scylitzes' chronicle, National Library, Madrid)

The *Comitatenses* units, which were then identified as the essence of the imperial army, consisted primarily of citizens of the empire. In a number of cases, they were organized along ethnic lines, creating military units of soldiers of common geographic origin. Thus, there existed units consisting of Isaurians (from Isauria, in Asia Minor), Thracians, Illyrians, Armenians and other nationalities. Often, though, the soldiers of these units were barbarians, mercenaries, or even prisoners of war, who usually served in regions far from those in which they had been captured. During Justinian's reign, the *Comitatenses* were divided into five armies. Two of them, the soldiers of which were also called *Praesentales*, because they served under the direct presence of the emperor, were stationed in Constantinople. Each of the remaining three armies was stationed in Illyria, Thrace, and the provinces of the East. Also during Justinian's reign, a further army was created in the province of Armenia and new units were raised in the new western provinces. In certain cases, the *Comitatenses* lost their mobility and were stationed in regions close to the borders in order to support and strengthen the effete guards of the *Limitanei*. In other provinces, including Egypt, the *Comitatenses* lost their battle worthiness through inactivity, because their provinces were never threatened. In addition, the *Comitatenses* of that time were considered inferior in military performance to the *Bucellarii* mercenary units. In fact, the Ostrogoth mercenaries, during the Italian campaign, contemptuously called the soldiers of the *Comitatenses* units "Greeks" as opposed to the term "Romans," with which all the empire's citizens identified.

During Justinian's time, the *Ballistarii*, those troops operating the catapults, constituted separate units. Their name emanated from the term "ballista," meaning stone-throwing catapult. Those units were stationed in the empire's major cities and were under the command of a local dignitary, the *Pater Civitatis* ("father of the city"). This same dignitary was also responsible for those who worked in the state *fabricenses* ("weapon industries") under his command. The larger infantry divisions, however, possessed their own catapult units.

SENIOR CAVALRY OFFICER OF THE EASTERN ROMAN EMPIRE (475 AD – 500 AD)
This particular illustration is based on "The Four Seasons" mosaic in Corinth, and depicts the equipment of a senior Greek or Roman officer of the Scholae *army corps.*
He wears the famous "muscular" cuirass, metal shoulder guards, segmented arm defences and carries a round shield with scaled surface (once the symbol of the Praetorian guard – the imperial bodyguard unit that ceased to exist after the Battle of the Milvian Bridge). (uniform research and reconstruction by Christos Giannopoulos)

Also during this time, local militias, which protected the cities and the surrounding countryside, supplemented the military forces of the Byzantine Empire. The empire's major cities, including Constantinople, Antioch, and Alexandria, had militias organized by the hippodrome factions. These factions exerted powerful political and social influence and participated in the protection of their city by organizing units of militiamen, night watchmen, and fire fighters. Similar units also existed in the smaller cities, although it is unknown if these constituted a permanent regular force or were just citizen groups who were exceptionally recruited for the defense of a besieged city, as happened in Rome and Milan during the Gothic Wars. By contrast, in the countryside, the militia units were more permanent with their basic mission being the protection of certain susceptible areas. For example, reports exist of militiamen guarding the area of the Thermopylae Pass.

The local *Magistri Militum* had overall command of the *Comitatenses* units. These dignitaries were considered supreme in the military as well as the social hierarchy and, as it was used in the Eastern Roman Empire, the importance of the office was reflected in the honorary titles they held. They were titled *Illustres* ("splendid"), *Gloriosi* ("glorious") or *Gloriosissimi* ("most glorious"). During Justinian's reign, the empire initially had five, later at least six *Magistri Militum*. Two *Magistri Militum Praesentales* were situated in Constantinople with command of the two *Comitatenses Praesentales* units stationed there. A further two protected the empire's Balkan borders with the *Magister Militum per Illyricum* commanding the *Comitatenses* units of the western Balkans and the *Magister Militum per Thracias* the corresponding *Comitatenses* units in the eastern Balkan region. The latter was very close to Constantinople and under the jurisdiction of the two *Magistri Militum Praesentales* positioned there. This arrangement prevented military power being concentrated in, or around the capital in the hands of just one dignitary, which could prove dangerous for the emperor. Another dignitary, the *Magister Militum per Orientem*, initially administered all the eastern provinces. However, in 528 AD, his jurisdictional region was split by the creation of the office of the *Magister Militum per Armeniam*, who was situated in Theodosioupolis (modern Erzurum inTurkey), with his jurisdiction covering the eastern borders of the empire from the Black Sea coasts to Martyropoli (modern Silban in Turkey), east of Amida (modern Diyarbakir in southeastern Turkey). Following the subjugation of Vandal state, the office of *Magister Militum Africae* was created in 534 AD.

In the border provinces, the administration was carried out by the *Duces* who were under the immediate jurisdiction of the corresponding *Magistri Militum*. The *Duces* commanded all the military units stationed in their province and were permanently characterized by the honorary title *Spectabilis* ("spectacular"). During Justinian's reign, the number of both the *Duces* and the *Magistri Militum* increased. The rank of the commanding officer of Armenia, for example, which earlier was a *Dux*, emerged as *Magister Militum* with five *Duces*, who shared the administration of the border regions, under his command.

The mercenaries

The *Bucellarii* were, as in the past, the personal military units of various generals. As time passed, they were also called by other names, including

Doryphoroi or *Hypaspistai*. Every important military official had an armed escort consisting of *Bucellarii*, a practice that was also progressively adopted by holders of political office. The number of men in these personal mercenary units became, in some cases, particularly large. For example, in 540 AD, Belisarius had a private army of 7,000 *Bucellarii* at his disposal. It is also reported that the *Magister Militum per Armeniam* ("military commander of Armenia") had 1,000 *Bucellarii*, while Narses, during the final period of the war in Italy, had 300. The *Bucellarii* were considered part of the particular dignitary's staff, along with the servants and other employees, dependent on him. Their commanding officer was the person in charge of all the dignitary's personnel, called *Maiordomus* ("Major of the Palace"). There was also the *Optio*, the person responsible for paying the soldiers' salaries. For the *Bucellarii*, the dignitary who paid them was their employer and military leader. They carried out his commands, fought when required, afforded him protection and, in return, he granted them everything they needed and imposed disciplinary punishments when necessary. The *Bucellarii*, however, also owed formal obedience to the emperor, to whom they swore fealty, as did the soldiers of the regular army.

The national origin of the *Bucellarii* varied, as they came from various tribes both within and without the empire. Their common origins, however, created common feelings and, thus, a kind of solidarity. These soldiers, although mercenaries, were considered elite and demonstrated their value through their richly embellished arms. The *Bucellarii*, during Justinian's time, were exclusively cavalrymen as, from that time, it was the cavalry that played the decisive role on the battlefield, usually undertaking the more critical offensive missions during a battle. The promotion of a soldier to *Bucellarius* was a tremendous boost for the best of those serving in the regular army. The *Foederati* and *Comitatenses* units followed in importance. This proves that, during Justinian's reign, the imperial army's dependence on mercenaries had not diminished, although Theodosius I's extremes were finally avoided. The use of mercenaries, however, had already begun to change the empire's military structure in a rather fundamental way. Many of the era's successful generals began their careers as *Bucellarii*, while the assignment of the administration of a regular army division to some *Bucellarius* was a frequent occurrence.

Mosaic illustration of the fortifications and port of Ravenna. (St. Apollinaire's Church, Ravenna)

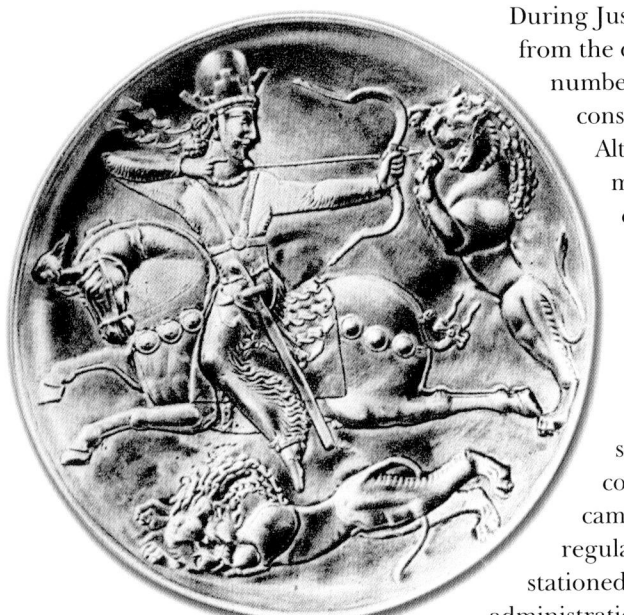

During Justinian's reign, the *Foederati* had come a long way from the disorganized barbarian units of earlier times. Their number had increased and it is very probable that they constituted half the empire's total military forces.

Although these units continued to consist of barbarian mercenaries, they were, however, based on the empire's military organization. The *Foederati* were considered elite soldiers and maintained the same privileges as the remainder of the soldiers of the Eastern Roman Empire. They consisted of units of cavalry and infantry and were used as guard units for certain regions or to take part in battles and other military operations. If their duty was to protect some region, they acted on the orders of the local commanding officers. When participating in campaigns, they came under the command of the regular army officers. As a large number of them were stationed in Constantinople, a special dignitary for their administration was constituted under the title *Comes Foederatorum*. They were also allowed to practice their own religion, a Christian sect based on the doctrine of Arius. Among the Germanic peoples this particular sect was widespread but, within the empire, it was, for the most part, persecuted. This concession to their faith, while serving the emperor, constituted a very significant privilege, especially during a period when religion was considered of particular importance. The *Foederati* usually came from specific nations that were renowned for their fighting qualities. When possible, the empire preferred to use them far from their home regions. Thus, in the wars against the Persians in the east, Goths, Heruli, and Huns were used, while, during the Italian campaign, the Byzantines used Heruli, Huns, and other races, the origin of whom remains obscure.

Illustration of a Persian king hunting lions dressed as a mounted archer. The extraordinary ability and skill of the Persians in the use of bows compelled the Byzantines to adjust their tactics and develop equally combat effective archer units. (Hermitage Museum, St. Petersburg)

In addition to the *Foederati* there were also the units of the "Allies". These "Allies" were barbarian races that had reached some kind of agreement with the empire. Their basic mission was to protect the empire's borders in those areas where their own state had common borders with it. In the event of war, they served in separate units under the command of their leaders. The "Allies" were paid an agreed salary or awarded special gifts. In some instances, their leaders were included in the empire's military hierarchy and awarded a Roman military rank. The Byzantine Empire particularly developed this kind of alliance and many peoples, including the Goths of Crimea, the Alans of the Caucasus, the Heruli and the Gepids (Germanic peoples), the Mauritanians, and even future enemies of the empire, such as the Lombards, the Avars and the Arabs accepted to participate in them. The empire's policy of accepting these peoples as allies actually led to them moving closer to her borders. Thus, the Lombards moved to Pannonia, in the northwestern regions of the Balkans, and the Avars from the northern Caucasus moved to the northern banks of the Danube. In time, however, these barbarian races turned out to be treacherous allies and mortal enemies of the empire, from whose control they were to wrest several important provinces.

*ROMAN (EARLY BYZANTINE) INFANTRY OFFICER
IN BATTLE DRESS (6TH CENTURY AD)
The warrior depicted here is one of the many thousand
German mercenaries who served in the armies
of the eastern Roman Empire. Characteristic elements
of his national identity are the* seax **German type**
of dagger hanging from his belt, **the** *francisca* **type**
of heavy battle-axe and the **wide** *periskelis* **(kind**
*of trousers that the eastern Germans introduced to their
clothing habits influenced by the Iranian-speaking
nomads of the steppe). (uniform research
and reconstruction by Christos Giannopoulos)*

The organization of the military units

By Justinian's time the organization of the units of the imperial army had been simplified. The basic military unit was the *numerus* ("number"). This term was ascribed to any kind of unit and, initially perhaps, referred to its pay-list, in which were recorded those who served in it. A complete *numerus* numbered 500 men although it also often covered larger or smaller units. In reality, each *numerus* covered from 200 to 400 men, although the number was nearer 300. This happened because a number of soldiers were occupied with administrative duties or were excused duty due to reasons of health. Another common practice by the military governors was to divide the men into more units than that which regularly corresponded with the actual number of their forces. This was so that any potential enemy would see more unit emblems and thus think that the Roman army was bigger than it was in reality. Each *numerus* was divided into *centuries*, with the latter being further divided into *decuries* that had a doctor and a priest, as well as a number of military servants who were at the disposal of the soldiers with the necessary amount of money. A *Tribunus* or *Comes* was the commanding officer of the *numerus* with a *Vicarious* assisting him in carrying out his duties. The terms *Tribunus* and *Comes* were used without discrimination in order to indicate the same degree of seniority. If a *numerus* was stationed in a city, then its commanding officer supplemented his rank with the name of this city. When a *numerus* was providing protection to a fortress, then its commanding officer, as commander of the garrison, was also called *Praepositus Castri*. Quite often he was also called *Praepositus* in the same way that, in the modern armies, there is a general term for "commander."

Each unit had its own emblem (*bandon*, a word from the Gothic term *bandwa*), which was carried by an elite soldier, the *Bandoforus* or *Draconarius*. The term *bandon* progressively lent its name to the military unit that carried this symbol, and was established finally during later centuries. Thus, the term *numerus* was gradually replaced with the term *bandon* or the Greek terms *tagma* ("batallion") or *arithmos* ("number"). The unit's standard *(bandon)* was particularly important for the soldiers when going into battle, as they marched behind it. By ordering the standard to move, the commanding officer in reality ordered the whole unit to follow it. For this reason, the standard bearer carrying it had to be experienced and brave, as any mistake could lead to serious consequences.

The *Strategikon*, an essay on military strategy that has been accredited to the Emperor Maurice (582 AD – 602 AD), constitutes a primary source for the organization of large military units during the 6th century. According to this work, the *moira* was a larger unit than the *numerus*, and was under the command of a *Dux*, who was also called by the Greek name *Moirarches* or *Chiliarchos*. The word *moira* is also found in the historical sources under the names of *agmen* (plural *agmina*) or *lochos* ("company"). A *moira* totaled some 3,000 men. Three *moiras* constituted a *meros* ("division," in the plural *mere*), under the command of a *Merarchos* ("divisional commander") or *Stratelate* (leader of the army). The total force of a *meros* could vary from 3,000 soldiers up to 6,000 or even 7,000 troops. Three *mere* constituted an army, under the command of a general. According to Maurice's *Strategikon*, a small army consisted of 5,000 men, a medium-sized one 5,000 - 15,000, with a large one as much as 20,000 - 24,000 including cavalry and infantry units.

It is difficult to calculate the total numerical force of the imperial army during Justinian's reign. The sixth-century historian Agathias wrote that the army muster was 150,000 soldiers and was scattered across a number of regions. He went on to write that this number was too small to be able to offer adequate protection to the empire. The size of this force becomes even more inadequate when Justinian's wars of expansion were taken into consideration. In 530 AD, Belisarius, as *Magister Militum per Orientem*, had 25,000 soldiers under his command, with which he had to face 40,000 Persians. The central military administration perceived the problem, however, and tried progressively to correct it.

Thus, in 554 AD, the empire disposed 50,000 soldiers against 60,000 Persians along its eastern borders. Generally speaking though, the manning of the eastern borders was relative to the course of the campaigns in the West. For example, in 533 AD – 534 AD, Belisarius destroyed the kingdom of the Vandals with 18,000 soldiers, the largest contingent of which came from the eastern provinces. With the subsequent occupation of the Vandal state, the empire was able to recruit the defeated enemy as mercenaries and, as a result, release Roman troops for military service in the East. However, not all the experienced soldiers that assisted in the subjugation of the Vandals returned home. Quite a large number remained in Africa in order to consolidate the imperial power. It is impossible, though, to estimate the exact number of barbarian mercenaries used by the empire at that time.

Justinian's imperial guard consisted of 10,000 soldiers, who were divided into various units. These were called *Excubitores* ("excubitors"), *Scholae Palatinae* or *Scholares* (in Latin, their Greek name was *scholarioi*), *Candidati* ("white-robed"), *Protectores* ("protectors") and *Scribones*. The *Excubitores*, created in the 5th century as a fighting unit by the Emperor Leon I the Thracian (457 AD – 474 AD),

Manuscript, dating from the beginning of the 6th century, showing a battle scene. Although it represents a scene from the Trojan Wars, each side appears to be carrying weapons of the era in which the manuscript was produced. (Ambrosian Library, Milan)

Ivory diptych representing Stilicho, his wife and child. Stilicho carries a spear, shield and sword. (Cathedral Museum, Monza, Italy)

totaled 300 men. Emperor Justin I (518 AD – 527 AD), Justinian's uncle and predecessor, before his ascent to the throne was commanding officer of the *Excubitores*, as the *Comes Excubitorum*. Members of the *Scholae Palatinae*, also called *Scholares*, were divided into seven units and had reached a total of up to 3,500 men. Justin I added another 2,000 soldiers to the *Scholae*, although Justinian later restored the unit to its original size. It is very likely that, during Justinian's reign, the *Scholae* had, to a great extent, lost their military character and become units carrying out primarily ritual duties. In certain cases, however, soldiers from the *Scholae* units took part in battles and campaigns. The *Excubitores* and the *Scholares* constituted the core of the emperor's bodyguard and participated in all the palace's rituals. Forty elite *Scholares* constituted the *Candidati* unit ("white-robed"), who were called thus due to the color of their clothing.

The *Protectores* were divided into *Protectores* and *Protectores Domestici*. The *Protectores Domestici* was considered superior and was called *Praesentales* if they served in Constantinople, or *Deputati*, if they served elsewhere. The *Protectores* were divided into units that were also called *Scholae* and constituted units of infantry or cavalry. The commanding officers of these units were titled *Primicerii*. The number of troops in the *Protectores Domestici Praesentales* was approximately 200, although

LOW RANKING OFFICER OF THE DANUBE
LEGIONS DURING THE REIGN
OF JUSTINIAN (6th CENTURY AD)
*The officer illustrated wears a Gothic
or Frankish style composite helmet (spagenhelm),
a chain mail breastplate, a yellow cloak
with coloured insignia patches indicating
his rank (this type of cloak was known
as a "Bulgarian sagion," meaning short cloak),
a long spear, a Frankish throwing axe (fransisca),
a northern German* seax *single-edged knife
and a heavy sword (not visible in the
illustration). (uniform research and
reconstruction by Christos Giannopoulos)*

the precise number of the rest is unknown. In the past, simple *Protectores* constituted a fighting unit of the emperor's bodyguard. By Justinian's time, however, they had lost their military nature and dealt exclusively with court duties. Of the *Scribones* unit little is known. While they constituted an armed group, it is unknown if they were considered a separate unit of the emperor's bodyguard or simply the *Excubitores* officer cadre. What is known is that it was primarily the *Scribones* who undertook important, sensitive missions.

The officers and soldiers in the 6th century

Officer selection was carried out by their superiors and then formally ratified by the emperor, who had the exclusive right to nominate the generals. Junior officer ranks were offered to soldiers who had served long and successfully. In certain cases, the junior officers came from the *Scholae* of the Emperor's Bodyguard *(scholae palatinae)* or the *Bucellarii*. In theory at least, there was no hindrance for any soldier to ascend through the ranks. Characteristic of this is the case of Emperor Justin I (518 AD – 527 AD), Justinian's uncle and predecessor. Justin began his career as a simple *Excubitor* and then emerged as *Dux*, then, it appears, as *Vicarious* ("second in command") to a *Magister Militum*, next as commanding officer of the *Excubitores (comes excubitorum)* unit and, finally, ascending the throne as emperor. The *Bucellarii* could rise to prominence either via command of a unit of other *Bucellarii* or through their incorporation into the hierarchy of the regular army.

Generals were divided into two categories, depending on how they were nominated. Some of them, whether citizens of the empire or foreigners, had been selected from the ranks of the regular army or the *Bucellarii* after a long service. The others gained their generalships either through their personal relationship with the imperial family, by virtue of personal favoritism or the political conditions at the time. These considerations, in certain cases, overshadowed or at least equaled the value or military abilities of the officer. In some extraordinary cases, the leader of the entire military forces of a campaign was given the title of

One of Rome's gates, this one was reconstructed by Belisarius during his Italian campaign.

Strategos-autocrator (meaning general holding absolute control). This title gave him absolute power as far as the conduct of war, the administration of the military forces, and the regions in which the operations were carried out, were concerned. The *Strategos-autocrator* functioned as a direct representative of the emperor himself. The first to receive this title was Belisarius, on the occasion of his departure for the campaign against the Vandals in 533 AD, and he retained it until the spring of 540 AD, when he was recalled to Constantinople and his administration was then divided into three parts, the most important of which was then taken over by a *Magister Militum*. The situation in Italy, however, soon proved that a single central administration with absolute power was required. The title of *Strategos-autocrator* was, however, very important and represented so much power that very few attained it. Apart from

Belisarius, the title of *Strategos-autocrator* was also held by Germanus, Justinian's cousin, when commander-in-chief during the Italian campaign, Narses, who completed the defeat of the Ostrogoth state, and Justin, Germanus' son and Justinian's nephew, for the administration of the eastern borders campaign. The authority and power of the *Strategos-autocrator* was, in all probability, similar to that of an *Exarch*.

The career path of the most notable military leader during this period, Belisarius, followed a very mixed course in his military service and in his relationship with the Court. This led him first to superior ranks and the emperor's favor and then to dishonorable recall from service and contempt. Whatever the direction, it was without doubt, very distinctive. Belisarius began his career as Justinian's *doryphoros (bucellarius)*, before the latter became emperor and throughout his time as heir and adviser to his uncle, Justin I. As a *Bucellarius*, he took over the administration of a campaign in Persarmenia after which Justin I named him *Dux* of Mesopotamia. In 529 AD, after Justinian had ascended the throne, Belisarius emerged as *Magister Militum per Orientem*, a title he held until 542 AD, although, simultaneously, he was also occupied on other fronts. In 531 AD, following a defeat by the Persians this title was revoked for a while. However, it was soon reinstated and he was assigned to the occupation of Africa (533 AD – 534 AD), followed by the administration of the campaign against Italy (535 AD – 540 AD), was again under the title of *Strategos-autocrator*.

In 540 AD, Belisarius was recalled from Italy but was soon in action again, this time against the Persians in the East (541 AD – 542 AD). However, during his absence he was accused of conspiring against the Emperor, recalled to Constantinople in 542 AD and stripped of all authority. It did not take him long to regain the Emperor's confidence and to be awarded the honorary title of *Comes Sacri Stabuli*, which was, however, inferior to the titles he had previously held. Under this title, he was assigned once again to the administration of the army in Italy (544 AD – 549 AD), although, in reality, he held the authority of a *Strategos-autocrator*. Returning from Italy in 549 AD, he was again awarded the title of *Magister Militum per Orientem*, although this was never actually put into effect and he remained in Constantinople conducting various honorary duties in the Emperor's Bodyguard. In 551 AD he withdrew, but still continued practicing certain auxiliary duties in the capital. A few years later, in 559 AD, he was, specially, assigned to command the troops mustered to intercept a raid by the Kutrigur Huns, who had reached the gates of Constantinople. His victory over the Huns was his final success. Afterwards he was, once again, in disgrace, due to an alleged new conspiracy against the Emperor. However, just before his death in March 565 AD, he was received back into the Emperor's favor. He and Justinian, with whom his life and career was irrevocably intertwined, both died in the same year. During his lifetime he had also been honored with the titles of *Patrician* and, in 535 AD, that of *Consul*, following his success in Africa. Many other military leaders of that era, either rising through the ranks of the citizens of the empire or from those of the barbarian mercenaries, had similar careers although none attained such high peaks or such low troughs.

The recruiting of soldiers usually took place in different ways, depending on the unit for which the recruits were intended. Generally speaking, however, two methods of recruitment were frequently applied, these also depending on the requirements of the particular time. The first was the regular and ongoing recruitment with the aim of replacing unit attrition resulting from the continuous wars; the second was the extraordinary recruitment, which, during Justinian's reign, became more frequent due to the perpetual military campaigns of the empire and the additional need for the protection of the new provinces in the West. The recruitment of the citizens of the empire became henceforth only voluntary as, it appears, that the previous century's laws on conscription had been revoked. Military service was, however, to a large extent hereditary and the majority of citizens serving in the imperial army were from families of military men. The minimum age for a man to be accepted into imperial army units was 18. As in the past, certain categories of people, including slaves, liberated slaves and their offspring, people who worked as employees at the courts of various local governors *(cohortales)*, criminals *(coloni adscripticii)*, those working in the administration services of the cities *(curiales)*, idolaters, Jews, and heretics were excluded from military service.

In 528 AD or 529 AD, Justinian also prohibited the recruitment of those who owned commercial enterprises, but allowed those who had already been recruited to remain in the army on condition that they immediately abandon their commercial activities. Certain exceptions pertaining to the prohibition of the recruitment of slaves were also invoked. A slave could join the army, on condition that his master was aware of it. By the 6th century, however, the Roman army's old distrust of the use of slaves had been overcome, as they had followed their masters on campaign and, in a number of instances, had fought alongside them. This particular practice, that appears to have been imported into the Roman army by the Germanic tribes, had changed the discriminatory views to such an extent that a number of slaves were accepted even in the emperor's bodyguard. It is possible that Christianity played an important role in this change. The empire's new religion did not totally accept slavery so that, progressively, it had begun to be replaced by the milder institution of serfdom.

Another usual practice, as mentioned earlier, was the recruiting of captives, specifically in Italy. In certain cases, this was done as a result of torture, but it could also be the result of a final treaty between the empire and its defeated opponents. The units in which the recruited captives served are still unknown; however, they were usually included into the units of the *Foederati*. For security reasons, the Byzantine army usually deployed them in regions far from their place of origin. The Ostrogoths, who were employed in Italy against their fellow-countrymen, were an exception to this rule.

The recruitment took place at given times, perhaps once a year, and was carried out by special teams dispatched by the local governors. The recruits in the *Comitatenses* and *Limitanei* units received a written certification from Constantinople, ratifying their recruitment. The process of recruiting the *Foederati* was about the same. The *Bucellarii*, in contrast, were usually recruited by agreement with their leader or with individuals. For the emperor's guard, vacancies in the *Scholae Palatinae* ("palace schools") and in the *Protectores* were covered either by soldiers recalled for rest and recuperation or by military or political employees that were close to their final retirement from service. This was because these units performed, to a large extent, purely ceremonial functions. The *Excubitores*, on the other hand, who constituted a fighting unit, were selected by strict military criteria.

EXCUBITOR - EMPEROR'S BODYGUARD IN BATTLE DRESS
(6th CENTURY AD)
Uniform reconstruction of an elite, heavily armed foot soldier
from the time of Justinian, based on the texts of Corripus and
Theofylaktos. The soldier wears a lamellar cuirass (lorica lamellar),
a late-Roman cassis helmet (the helmets of those serving
in the palace were of a somewhat archaic shape
and manufactured from bronze or were gold-plated),
an old-style round shield (clipeus), a spear (hasta),
a seax German dagger, and a double axe (securis).
When the Excubitores accompanied the emperor
or high-ranking generals, they wore red tunics
and cloaks, belts adorned with gold
and red knee-high boots (cothurni).
When the bodyguards were
on palace duty, the cothurni
footwear were mid-calf length.
(uniform research
and reconstruction
by Christos Giannopoulos)

The soldiers' armament

During Justinian's reign, the imperial army troops had exceptionally high quality weapons, in the use of which they were continually and consistently trained. The most powerful part of the army was the cavalry and the bow was the most important weapon. The mounted arm was also trained to fight on foot. During their training and on campaign, particular emphasis was placed on the units' mobility. With an army so comparatively small in relation to the size of the empire, mobility ensured the possibility of covering larger areas as well as being able to withdraw quickly, in the case of its smaller forces having to be rescued, especially when faced with more powerful opponents. The cavalry was divided into lancers and archers. Of these two, the lancers undertook defensive missions having to do with the protection of other military units *(defensives)*, while the archers often had a more aggressive role; however, their roles could be reversed. The cavalryman wore a chain mail tunic, which gave him a degree of protection. In some instances, a steel breastplate or small plates of metal strengthened his armor. A helmet and metal greaves up to the knee usually supplemented the cavalryman's protective equipment. In his left hand he held a medium-sized shield and, in the right, a lance or bow. Sometimes he also carried a smaller shield hung across his back to afford further protection from the rear. On his right side hung a quiver of arrows, with a sword on his left. The horses also carried protective armor, at least over part of their body; initially, however, this was somewhat light, at least in the units of horse archers, in order to ensure greater speed and flexibility during battle. The lancers carried a long spear, called a *contus*, along with a bow, strung across their body. The mounted archers held the bow in their right hand, but they also carried one or more javelins that were lighter than the lancers' spear and these were also strung across their shoulders or in special sockets. While the archers' javelin was not very effective in close order battle, it could, nevertheless, be thrown at an opponent from a considerable distance.

The extensive use of the bow helped the Roman-Byzantine army of Justinian's time to avoid hand-to-hand battles with the Germanic tribes, who distinguished themselves by their aggressiveness and ferocity in this type of warfare. Over time, the Byzantine archers acquired expertise in the use of the bow comparable to those of the Persians and the other peoples who were famous for their effectiveness with this weapon, as far as its military use was concerned. They were capable of moving with great speed on their horses while launching arrows in every direction. Their technique, which was considered more effective than that of the Persians, was based on pulling the string of the bow up to the archer's right ear. This way the arrow acquired a force capable of penetrating even shields and breastplates within the bow's effective range. Furthermore, the ability of these archers can be better appreciated when one considers that they rode without stirrups and wore a body armor weighing approximately 16kgs.

The infantry was divided into heavy and light units. The heavy infantry was specifically intended for use at the most critical points of the battle array. According to Maurice's *Strategikon*, a soldier of the heavy infantry wore a chain mail tunic, helmet, greaves, a large shield, a sword (there was no regulation size for this), a long spear, a sling, a number of *martzobaboula* ("small lead-weighted darts") and, in certain cases, a heavy double-headed axe. The mission of the light infantry units was to screen the line of battle and they carried bows, quivers, javelins, slings, *martzobarboula* and small shields. By Justinian's reign, the infantry had lost to a large extent the formidable reputation that it had enjoyed during the previous centuries. The thinking that dominated the empire's generals at that time was the opinion that infantry units were only fit to play a secondary and auxiliary role in the conduct of a war and their primary mission was to take possession and consolidate territory already captured, not meet the enemy head-on. Belisarius was among the supporters of this tactical thinking and, indeed, he applied it during his African campaign of 533 AD – 534 AD. While the largest contingent of his forces during this campaign consisted of infantry units, Belisarius did not use them in any of the battles he fought. There were, however, generals who supported the opposite, such as Narses, who used infantry units extensively during the latter stages of the war in Italy.

The forces of the Allies fought using their own weapons, and their presence gave the Byzantine armies a marked diversity. In many cases, methods used by the barbarians were an invaluable source of inspiration for the empire's generals and led to innovations that involved a high degree of risk. The Heruli, for instance, fought without armor and helmets, using only their shield and a long cloak for protection. Their slaves, who were granted the right to use a shield if they proved themselves competent warriors, also fought alongside them. The Huns, who were used during most campaigns, were equal to the empire's best as far as mounted archery was concerned. During the same campaign, the Mauritanians rose to prominence because of their light javelinmen, who gave them the ability to move quite fast, thus, placing the enemy's slow-moving units at a disadvantage. The heavy cavalry of the Goths was equally successful in the East. Goth horsemen defeated the Persian cavalry by using the long spears at which the Germanic peoples were very adept.

Fortifications and sieges during the 6th century

Siege tower with battering ram at its lower level.

The defense of the empire's borders during the 6th century continued to rely on the same principles that were generally applied during Constantine's reign. The barbarians living near the borders played an important role in their protection, since they constituted the first line of defense against hostile raids. Behind them were the fortresses of the *Limitanei* and the forces of the *Comitatenses* that were able to move to any area under serious threat.

The frontier area no longer comprised a simple line of fortresses, which delimitated the border. The increased threat to the empire all along its borders had forced the imperial army to establish a defense network along the frontiers by developing a line of strongholds. The frontier fortifications differed depending on each particular region and the conditions that prevailed; however, there was one common element in all regions: the establishment of a road network along which reinforcements could be quickly moved to the threatened areas. The network of fortifications of certain frontier regions was so dense that, in the region of the Danube for example, all rural settlements possessed their own fortified tower or were built very close to a fortress.

Although the border regions constituted the empire's basic line of defense, important fortresses were found in all provinces. The Roman state no longer enjoyed the luxury of hoping it would manage to halt the hostile raids at its borders, so all provinces, even if far from the borders, had to be prepared to intercept barbarian incursions. Apart from the cities, powerful fortresses were built to protect vital rear areas such as passes, hills, and harbors. The fortifications were of various types, depending on the particular place they protected. There were also extensive fortified precincts in cities, including Constantinople, Nicaea, Thessalonica, Antioch, and Carthage. There also existed powerful military fortresses or even individual towers. The various fortresses and fortified settlements were also used as places of refuge for the residents of the countryside in times of danger. In addition, there were also fortresses constructed for private use (fortified monasteries or manors of landowners). Indeed, some of them were so immense, that in some instances during modern archeological excavations, it is difficult to distinguish between military and civil facilities of that period. When it was not possible for an entire monastery or manor to be fortified, those who could afford it often built a fortified tower, in order to use it as a refuge in the event of a hostile raid. The presence of walls actually became an essential element of urban life. One of the advantages of life in the city was, henceforth, the safety afforded by the walls. Justinian, whose name is associated with splendid buildings, showed considerable interest in the construction of fortifications or their upkeep where they already existed.

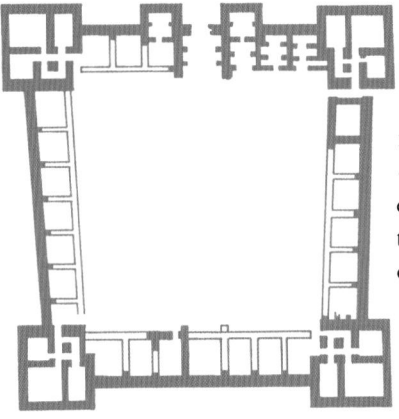

Ground plan of a typical quadriburgium *from the region of Jordan.*

The presence of fortresses, however, did not, by any means, ensure the empire's security. On the contrary, it forced the imperial army into a more static position and compromised flexibility in confronting its enemies. In 531 AD, the Persian King Kabades (Kavadh in Persian) succeeded in penetrating the empire's defensive line by the simple expedient of bypassing all the frontier fortresses. In 540 AD, the Persian King Khosrau I repeated the same tactic by a much bolder method and with even more surprising results. He launched a surprise invasion of the empire's territories, violating the peace treaty that had been signed between Persia and Justinian eight years earlier. The Persian army, having followed the right bank of the Euphrates River, bypassed all the important fortresses of the region and not only reached, but also captured Antioch before returning to its base. The Persian king then repeated the same tactic in each of the three succeeding years, until a renewed peace treaty was agreed in 545 AD. Similar problems also arose along the borders of the empire, especially in the northern Balkans and Italy, where barbarian invaders attempted to infiltrate its territories. Even the frontier line along the Italian Alps was, finally, unable to halt the Lombard invasion.

In the Balkans, various Germanic, Mongol, and Slavic tribes carried out frequent raids and they even managed to intrude deep into the territories of the Eastern Roman Empire, notwithstanding the presence of the fortresses positioned to halt them. The northern provinces of the region regularly fell victims to the barbarian invaders who, quite often, reached the Aegean coasts and even advanced further south. In 528 AD, the Bulgarians invaded Thrace. In 536 AD, the Gepids occupied Sirmium (modern day Sremska Mitrovica in northwest Serbia), one of the most important cities of the western Balkans, along with a large part of the nearby region. In 540 AD, a devastating Bulgarian raid once again laid waste to the regions of Thrace and Macedonia. In the province of Illyria, the Bulgarians occupied a total of 32 fortresses along with the city of

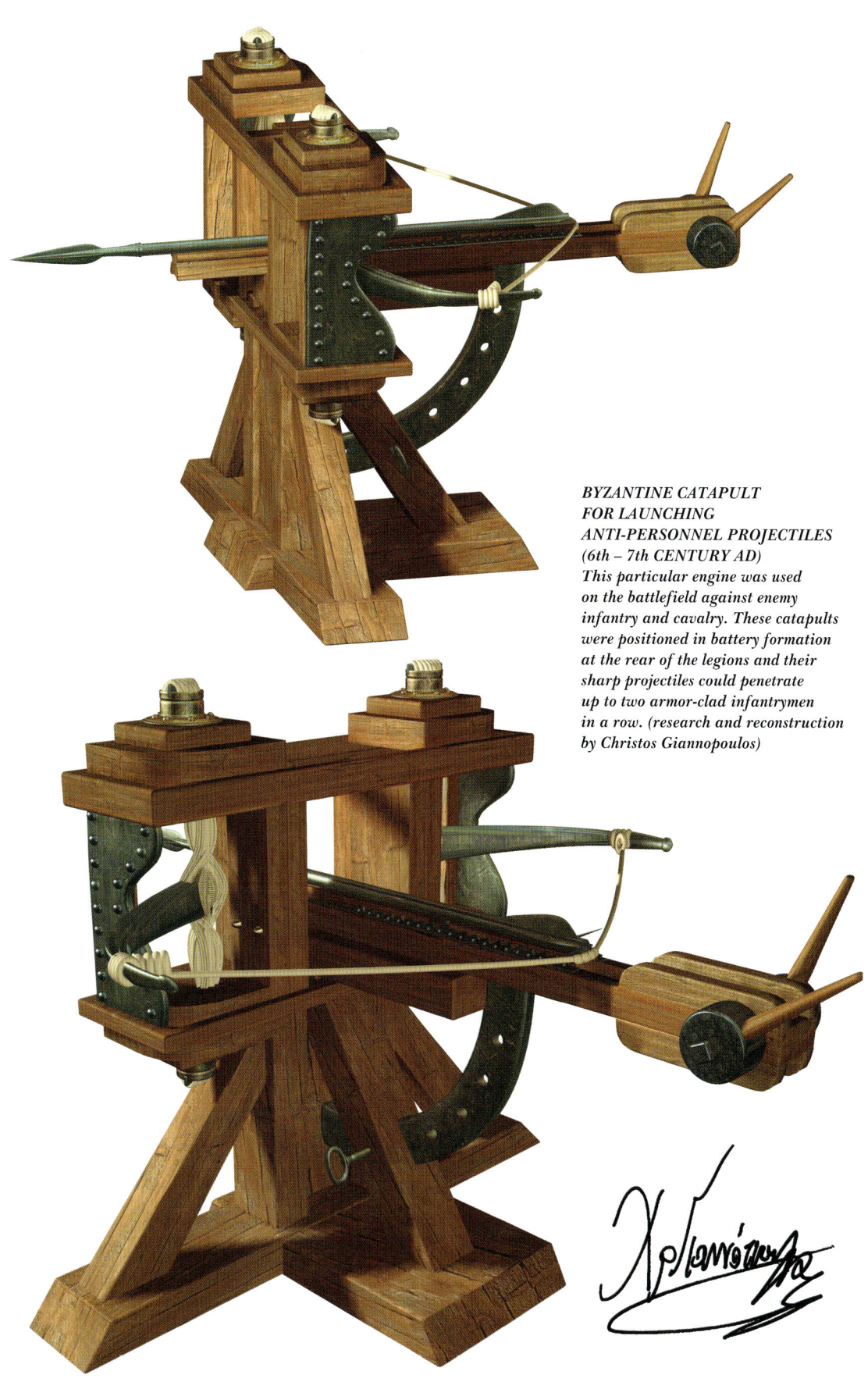

**BYZANTINE CATAPULT
FOR LAUNCHING
ANTI-PERSONNEL PROJECTILES
(6th – 7th CENTURY AD)**
*This particular engine was used
on the battlefield against enemy
infantry and cavalry. These catapults
were positioned in battery formation
at the rear of the legions and their
sharp projectiles could penetrate
up to two armor-clad infantrymen
in a row. (research and reconstruction
by Christos Giannopoulos)*

Kassandreia in Chalkidiki, which proved that the construction of fortifications did not constitute an absolute guarantee of security. In the spring of 559 AD, the Utrigur Huns, including groups of Bulgarians and Slavs, reached Thermopylae, while another large force of intruders was driven back by Belisarius just a few kilometers short of Constantinople.

The supplementary occupation of the imperial army with the construction of fortifications offered, in addition, important knowledge, as far as their defense or occupation were concerned. The siege and capture of a fortress was quite a demanding military operation requiring organization, technical knowledge, and special skills. Assaulting and occupying a fortified position by frontal attack was only used as an emergency with the majority of military commanders avoiding it, because of the increased danger and the probable heavy losses this would entail. Most successes in overcoming fortified cities were achieved through surrender by treaty or secret agreement with the besieged. Quite frequently it was also achieved through subterfuge. The city of Soura, on the empire's eastern borders, was captured when the inhabitants sent their archbishop to negotiate with the Persian King Khosrau I, who was investing it. Khosrau I received the archbishop and then granted him an honorary escort for his return to the city. The soldiers of the escort were, however, ordered to launch an unexpected attack when the gates of the city were opened for the archbishop, and keep them open for the Persian army, which had followed out of sight of Soura's defenders. In a number of instances, an invested city fell after a traitor had helped the besiegers. In most sieges, the besiegers' most powerful weapon was starvation, but this required time and necessitated that all the city's access routes be securely blockaded.

Roman army siege engines. (French 18th century engraving)

The capacity of a city or fortress to resist a siege depended on a number of factors, the most important being the quality of the fortifications. Inaccessible sites were ideal for the construction of a hypothetically impenetrable fortress. If the terrain surrounding the besieged city or fortress was difficult, this would prevent the approach of battering rams up to the walls. In contrast, cities or fortresses sited on a plain or any level terrain were more vulnerable, as the besiegers could get their siege engines right up to the walls. A particular danger for the besieged was if the region around the city or fortress offered the besiegers both sufficient pasture for their animals and abundant water sources.

The disadvantages of level ground in front of certain fortifications could be alleviated by the construction of necessary earthworks. A deep moat in front of the wall could prevent, or at least delay the approach of siege engines. Sometimes, to strengthen the effect of a moat, a rampart was constructed in front of the regular wall that considerably increased its perceived width, so that the enemy would also have to go over it before reaching the actual walls. Defenders were at a serious disadvantage if their fortress was surrounded by hills on which besiegers could position catapults and other war engines. In such cases, the defenders would attempt to alleviate the danger by increasing the height of the walls at specific points, by digging trenches around the sides of hills to obstruct the movement of siege engines, or, even more drastically, level entire hills.

A sufficient supply of food and fresh water was of vital importance for the besieged. Most of the empire's cities were supplied with water via aqueducts. The Justinian's Eastern Roman Empire continued the old Roman tradition of constructing impressive technical works to bring fresh water into the cities, even over long distances. During a siege, however, the besiegers could destroy part of the aqueduct that was outside the walls or poison the water source. To counteract this, reservoirs were built in each city to maintain a supply of water. Of course, the ideal solution for the besieged was the existence of a fresh water spring within the walls, although this was not possible in all cases. Moreover, if a well did exist, it was unlikely to be large enough to cover the needs of the besieged. A case in point is the siege by the imperial army of Urbino in Italy. The city's Ostrogoth guard initially satisfied their water requirements from a spring inside the walls. When, however, this spring ran dry through overuse, the Ostrogoths were forced to surrender. In other cases, secret water pipes were also used. For example, during the siege of Petra, the fortress's Persian defenders had constructed three overlying water pipes. The besieging imperial army managed to locate the two upper ones and cut them off, but did not, however, discover the existence of the third one until after the fortress finally fell.

The siege engines

During sieges, both the attackers and defenders used a large number of war engines as artillery. For the defense of the fortresses, *scorpions* (stone-throwing catapults) and *ballistae* (machines for launching javelins) were mainly used. These machines, which had double bowstrings, hurled larger and heavier missiles than those of individual archers. The *ballistae* were mainly anti-personnel weapons, which were able to penetrate breastplates from a long distance and often struck down an enemy file with one projectile. The *scorpions* were also used against enemy personnel but were, however, more effective in destroying fortifications and other heavy immobile targets. The engines for launching missiles were positioned on the towers or atop the walls in order to allow a wider firing angle. The stone throwers' disadvantage was that they could only fire straight ahead, thus covering just a limited area of the battlefield. *Lupi* (the word actually means "wolves") and *triboli* were also used. The *lupi* were wooden surfaces through which nails had been driven with their points facing out. These nails were called "wolf's teeth," which gave this machine its name. These surfaces were then supported on two stakes and then placed above the gates. When the enemy assaulted the gates, the defenders let the *lupi* fall on them, causing much death and injury. The *triboli* were small metal spikes. Each

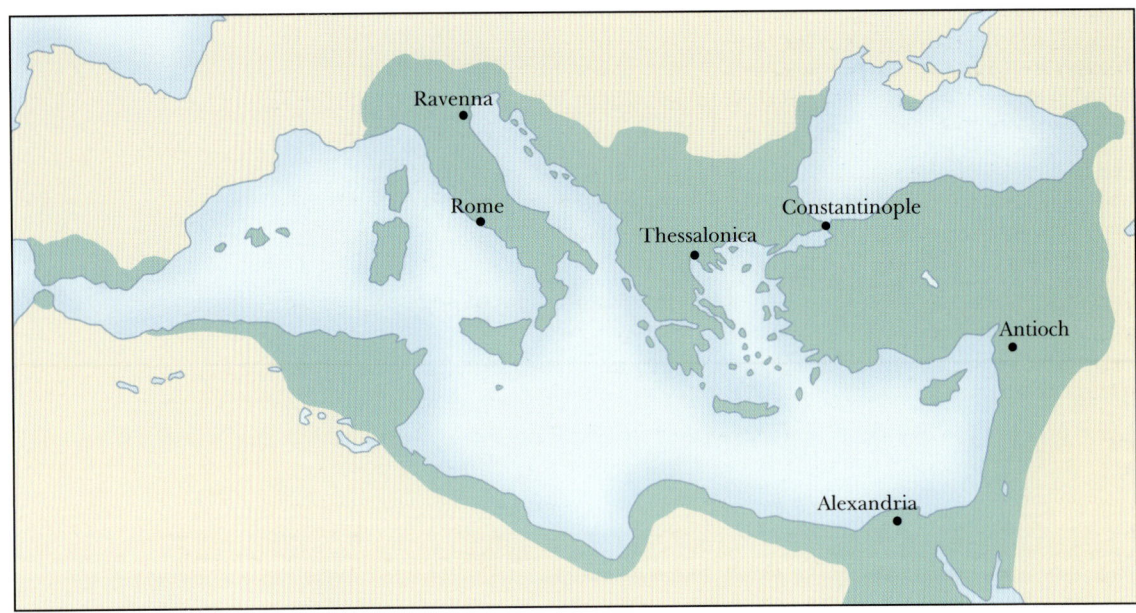

The Byzantine Empire during Justinian's time.

tribolus consisted of four spikes and were manufactured so that, no matter how it fell on the ground, one from these spikes pointed upwards. The use of the *triboli* thus constituted a means to delay or hinder the movement of troops and particularly animals. Their use, in combination with the war engines, proved to be particularly effective. When a group of attackers attempted to avoid the *triboli*, which slowed them down, they became an easy target for the *ballistae* and "scorpions."

The most common siege engine was the *krios* ("ram" in English and *aries* in Latin). The "ram" was a large movable deckhouse, made of wood and protected on the exterior by wet animal skins, which prevented it from being set alight. The ram was equipped with wheels for ease of movement. In its interior, usually at its lowest level, was a large wooden beam with a sharpened end for damaging a fortress' walls. Usually, the end of the beam was strengthened with metal, either in the form of an obelisk, or foursquare or, in some cases, the head of a ram. The beam was hung from the roof of the wooden deckhouse by chains. Thus, it could move freely back and forth and continuously strike a given point on the wall. A "ram" required around 50 men to move and operate it. It was an exceptionally heavy machine, and required level ground to be able to move it, as it was impossible to move on any incline or even over just small bumps. During Justinian's reign, a lighter battering "ram" was devised that could be transported on the backs of 40 men and, therefore, could be used even on uneven terrain. This "ram" had no wheels and the deckhouse, which protected the operators, was of much lighter construction.

When advancing on the walls of a besieged city or fortress for ramming or other purposes, attackers would take cover in deckhouses similar to those used for "rams." These deckhouses were called *chelones* ("turtles" in English and *testudina* in Latin), not only because of their shape and use, but also because of the movement of the "ram" beam back and forth that was reminiscent of the movement of a turtle's head. When ramming was not intended, "turtles" allowed engineers to approach the walls of the enemy fortification in order to start offensive operations such as digging to undermine them. Another variant

PROTOSTATES - ANTESIGNANIUS **FRONT RANK INFANTRYMAN (6th CENTURY AD)**
During the reign of Justinian, front rank troops, as well as those of the rearguard reserves, were issued with heavier armor and larger shields than the remainder of their colleagues. This particular soldier's mail armor covers almost the whole of his body, excluding his arms that in this instance are shown protected by segmented metal guards. His helmet sports a solid metal crest denoting some form of rank. His offensive weapons consist of a spiculum-type *javelin, a Celtic-style spear, a German-style single-edged* scrama-seax *knife and a broad bladed sword (not shown). (uniform research and reconstruction by Christos Giannopoulos)*

of the "turtle" was the *vinea* (a Latin word meaning "grapevine" or "gallery"), which was a moving deckhouse, under which the besiegers could move around the walls in safety.

To counteract these siege engines, the fortress's defenders often constructed a second moat, behind one that already existed. This auxiliary moat was located in the area between the rampart and the wall. In order to prevent the battering "rams" from striking the base of the walls, the defenders built up piles of earth in these areas, which prevented the head of the "ram" from coming into contact with the stones of the walls. Furthermore, the fortress's defenders created banks and humps on the ground around it in order to hinder the approach of hostile siege engines up to the walls. The defenders also used various means to protect the soldiers and the military machines inside the walls. Loopholes protected them from missiles that were fired horizontally, but not vertically. A solution was to use special, durable cloth that was unfolded over the defenders to provide protection. If these were unavailable, they even resorted to bed blankets although these were an afterthought and not particularly effective. Against the stones launched by the "scorpions," the best protection was to use nets made of thick ropes. These were used to cover the military equipment and so decrease the effect of the blows aimed at them.

During the sieges, battering towers were also used that were run up to the walls and carried war engines to a higher level than that of the walls so they could strike at the city's interior. In addition, these engines, offered better protection to those attempting to assail the base of the walls, the engineers units and operators of the "rams," who, covered by the "turtles," attempted to undermine the fortifications. The towers had square bases with sides between 9 - 15 meters in length. They were fitted with wheels in the base and were pushed up to the walls either by men or pulled by oxen. Each tower contained a number of levels. On the level closest to the bottom was, perhaps, a battering "ram" to strike the walls, whereas on the middle level there was a mobile bridge to allow the movement of attackers from the tower onto the walls of the besieged city and, finally, on the upper levels there was sufficient space for the ballistic machines ("scorpions" and *ballistae*) and the archers. A successful tower would, in theory, be higher than the walls it was meant to be used against, so that the assailants could attack the wall's defenders from a greater height.

These towers, despite being well constructed and covered with skins to prevent their being set alight by incendiary missiles, were not totally invulnerable to attack. The defenders could destroy a tower by launching a bold sortie against it. If they managed to eliminate the troops surrounding it, the tower could easily be set alight at its base. In some instances, the city's defenders used different raiding tactics. Small groups with shrouded oil lamps, which could not be clearly seen in the dark, descended the walls using ropes. These raiding parties then stealthily approached the battering machines and set them alight before returning to the fortress by the same route.

At the siege of Palermo in Sicily, Belisarius used battering towers in a very innovative way, transporting them to the walls by boat. This brilliant idea finally led to the capture of the city, proving that, during sieges, very often victory went to the protagonist who applied the most innovative methods, forcing his opponents to confront tactics they had never before faced. The Persians, in some instances, also used mounds instead of battering towers or a combination of both.

These mounds were built to the same, or even greater height than the city walls and acted as a base for the artillery. This technique was known earlier to imperial army engineers under the name *adgestum* ("pile"), however, no further detailed information exists on how it was applied.

During sieges, the engineers of the besieging force tried to undermine the walls by digging galleries beneath them. The defenders could detect them from a number of giveaway clues, such as the concentration of large amounts of soil at some point, a sure sign that excavations were taking place somewhere, or from strange sounds coming from beneath the ground. Usually the besiegers, in order to create confusion among the defenders, did not dig a single gallery, but instead dug a number of galleries, making their exact location more difficult to detect. When the besieged realized that galleries were being dug and had located their exact position, they could prevent further encroachment by digging a moat parallel to the wall and one meter in front of it. In this way, they could meet their opponents galleries and expel them using smoke. While digging their ditch, the defenders collected the soil and used it to create a mound in front of the ditch to protect their war engines. In this case, the existence of a ditch helped the defenders and prevented the besiegers from digging underground galleries. On a number of occasions, the opposing engineers met underground resulting in savage skirmishes. If the besiegers achieved their goal of reaching beneath the city walls undetected, they then attempted to destroy a portion of the walls, usually by setting fire to the timber that had been used to construct the galleries. The resulting collapse of the gallery caused part of the walls above it also to collapse. Following a collapse, the besiegers had to move quickly in order to enter the city through the gap that had been created in the fortifications. This operation was not always as successful as anticipated, however. Often the defenders, despite their surprise from the collapse of part of the walls, managed to stand their ground, drive back the attackers and then temporarily cover the gap by constructing a triangular rampart inside the city, in front of the point where the wall section had fallen.

Slavonic manuscript of Constantine Manasses' chronograph showing a Persian raid against a Byzantine city. On the left can be seen the Byzantine archers on the walls and, on the right, the Persian cavalry. (Apostolical Library, Vatican)

Battles during Justinian's time

The army's generals during Justinian's reign preferred to avoid head-to-head battles. They felt that this type of battle could prove dangerous and it was too risky to jeopardize any positive results of an extended campaign in a short conflict. Strategic thought during this period was based on the concept that the conduct of a war should be a thoroughly planned operation, in which even the smallest detail should be well thought-out. Within this context, there existed no room for risky operations. In the case of Justinian's generals being forced into a battle, and this not developing positively, retreat was imperative. The Roman – Byzantine army of that time did not consider retreat a shameful manoeuvre, especially when the battle had been definitely lost. On the contrary, in such a case, the military leaders were obliged to rescue as many of the forces under their command as they could. Moreover, the imperial army's limited numbers left little room for wasting its human resources. Indeed, during the campaign in Italy, Belisarius, addressing his soldiers, stressed that they should not try to avoid retreating, when there existed no other solution for the army's salvation.

Before the imperial army became involved in a battle, the configuration of the enemy's army, its competence, its level of training, the type of weapons and the morale of the troops would have been taken into consideration. If the commanding officer judged that conditions were encouraging enough, he could attempt a head-to-head battle. For the generals of that period, numerical superiority over the enemy did not necessarily constitute an essential condition; however, they preferred to avoid giving battle if conditions fell short of any of the afore-mentioned criteria. When an opponent deployed equal forces, they tried to gain a tactical advantage, either by forcing the enemy army to fight in a territory not of its choosing or cutting its supply lines. Splitting the enemy army into smaller groups and then eliminating them piecemeal was a very common Byzantine tactic. Belisarius was one of the foremost exponents of this tactic which, however, required the imperial army to have mobile forces, capable of being deployed in smaller groups and then also applying – apart from the methods of the regular army – unorthodox tactics, thus conducting a war of attrition. During the final stage of the war in Italy, the imperial army impeded the concentration of the Goths round Bologna by setting continuous ambushes. At the same time, more or less, the military forces that were sent to prevent a Slavic raid in the Balkans, being smaller than the invaders, did not offer an open battle but, instead, watched and harassed the enemy and exterminated foragers that wandered from the main body of the hostile forces.

When selecting an appropriate battlefield, the generals of the Eastern Roman Empire checked the area to ensure adequate room for maneuver for their forces and an acceptable route of retreat in case the battle did not develop positively. They preferred to offer battle on level, flat ground, because the cavalry, which constituted the army's main shock component during this period, could move more easily. Before the battle, the forces were arrayed mainly in three ways. The first involved three adjacent cavalry forces. In this case, the infantry forces were regularly used as reserves and took no part in the battle. This was the method preferred by Belisarius. For the second option, the cavalry were drawn up into two or three core units, with the infantry forces positioned as a second line. In the third option, the infantry was positioned in the center of the battle formation with the cavalry forces on both flanks. During the organization of the battle formation, the soldiers were deployed together by origin and category (*Foederati*, *Bucellarii*, barbarian mercenaries). Other solutions concerning the configuration of the battle formation were not excluded, but depended on current circumstances. In these types of formation, the empire's opponents replied with equivalent levels of organization, especially if they practiced some kind of sophisticated military tactics. The Persians in the East, as well as the Vandals and Ostrogoths in the West, drew up their forces for battle on an organized front. In contrast, the other barbarian enemies of the empire launched their attacks in a totally disorganized manner. Notably strange, though, was the Mauritanian battle formation, which, on one occasion, dismounted and took cover behind their prostrate camels.

Typically, a degree of army preparation took place before a battle. A Mass would be held, initially for the general and then for the army's troops. The priests, who served the camp, first blessed the soldiers, the general then followed this with a rousing speech. The trumpets then sounded the signal for the start of the battle. Following this, the army's standards were raised and the soldiers walked to their positions shouting their battle cries. As the forces left the camp, the priests and officers shouted, "Lord Jesus Christ have mercy on us" to which the soldiers replied, *Deus nobiscum* ("God be with us"). Usually the battle began at dawn and continued for many hours, sometimes for the entire day. In a number of instances, some generals would break these rules, hoping to catch the enemy unprepared. At Dara in Mesopotamia, the Persians attacked the imperial army at noon, hoping the soldiers would either be eating or resting, confident that they would not give battle that day. The Persians were proved correct with the Byzantines being initially surprised; however, they immediately managed to form up and, eventually, the Persian attack failed. In order to avoid any nasty surprises by the enemy, Narses, while waiting for the final battle against the Ostrogoths at Busta Gallorum in Italy, ordered his troops to take a light lunch and not remove weapons during the day. In fact, this critical battle, the victory of which ensured the final dominance of the empire in Italy, began at midday and continued until late in the evening.

Part of the wall constructed during the Justinian's reign on the Isthmus of Corinth to protect the Peloponnesus from raids by the barbarians who had infiltrated into the Balkans. These raids were made possible by the weakening of the Balkan borders by moving military units and allocating huge amounts of money for the occupation of Italy.

Often individual combats between selected champions preceded the battle. The purpose of those duels was for elite soldiers to display their fighting skills while boosting the morale of the rest of the army. In Dara in 530 AD, Bouzes, a capable soldier belonging to the *Magister Militum's* entourage, succeeding in killing two Persians in successive duels that lasted so long, that, by the end, the opposing armies were forced to withdraw as it was already too late and the battle took place on another day. Before the battle against the Vandals in north Africa, a Hun mercenary of Belisarius' army advanced in front of the lines of his battle formation, and challenged any elite Vandal soldier to fight him. The Hun carried out this action because, he claimed, it was his family's tradition that no family member could participate in any battle if it was not first opened by a relative. In this instance, however, no one from the Vandal's battle formation took up the challenge, giving him, and the remainder of Belisarius' army, the opportunity to show contempt for their enemy. As far as the deciding battle for the occupation of Italy at Busta Gallorum was concerned, this was also preceded by some duels that resulted in a positive outcome for the Byzantine army. This was followed by a war dance by Totila, leader of the Ostrogoths, with both sides as spectators. Totila danced, not so much to make an impression, but because he was waiting for reinforcements and wished to delay the outbreak of hostilities as long as possible.

During the battles and, indeed, all the military operations carried out during that period, the cavalry was considered the more powerful arm, especially the units of mounted archers whose actions could turn the tide in favor of the imperial army. Belisarius considered the cavalry to be of paramount importance, and usually excluded his infantry forces from the head-to-head confrontations. This tactic, indeed, had in certain cases, caused a negative reaction from certain officers, who protested that he had offended their troops. They actually

Section of the Thessalonica fortifications.

A medal struck to commemorate the subjugation of the Vandal state in North Africa. One side shows Justinian wearing a breastplate and helmet, while on the other, the mounted Emperor is depicted following Nike (Greek goddess of victory). (Monetary Museum, Athens)

reminded him that the Roman Empire had been created thanks to the power of its infantry. Despite their protests, whenever Belisarius used infantry units in battle he deployed them in positions of minor importance, simply covering the flanks and rear of the horsemen. By doing this, Belisarius prevented any possible encircling movement by the enemy while also preventing the cavalry from retreating without a direct order. Many other generals during the 6th century held the same opinion about the use of infantry.

The basic factor determining the predominance of the imperial army in a battle was its discipline. At that time, though, the phenomenon of severe mass indiscipline was endemic and this possibly constituted an additional factor leading the generals to avoid entering a possible pitched battle. This indiscipline, in some cases, emanated from the soldiers' dissatisfaction with the army's dysfunctional resupply system and the long delays in the payment of salaries and gifts. Quite often, it was the generals themselves who created problems owing to personal antagonisms and rapaciousness. Indeed, the Imperial Court deliberately inflamed these personal jealousies with the aim of imposing its favorites in the administration. A case in point was Narses' expedition in Italy in 538 AD that was characteristically significant. Narses was sent to the region as the chosen of the imperial Court and attempted to favor those officers who supported him or other persons of the Court. Similar behavior led to greater indiscipline across all ranks of the military hierarchy. In some instances, the troops' indiscipline resulted in open revolt, as happened in North Africa in 536 AD and Italy in 540 AD. Often though, the position of the generals was precarious, as they did not hold absolute control of the troops under their command, while their junior officer cadres were fragmented due to personal antipathies and behaved badly. The distribution of plunder, especially between the units of the regular army and the foreign mercenaries or the allies, also constituted another reason for dispute. During the campaign in Mesopotamia, the leader of the Saracen allies did not dare to appear before Belisarius, because he was afraid that he would be commanded to hand over part of the plunder that he had accumulated. Despite the problems that arose at times, the army of the Eastern Roman Empire remained effective. Justinian's generals usually managed to carry out the missions assigned them, despite the extreme difficulties involved in the administrative tasks they confronted. (Most of the above mentioned facts concerning Justinian's army can be found in *I Bizantini e la Guerra* by Giorgio Ravegnani, Roma, 2004).

The army
of the Byzantine Empire
in the Middle Byzantine Era
(642 AD – 1204 AD)

The survival of Byzantium
amidst a throng of foes

The "themes" during the 7th century. The thematic borders in the Balkan peninsula are obscure due to constant Slavic raids. The "thematic" organization was the basis of the Byzantine military and administrative system for more than four centuries and was historically linked to the empire's "golden era."

The organization of the themes

The end of Heraclius' reign found the empire in a very difficult position. The provinces of Syria, Palestine, and Egypt had been lost, while the Arabs continued their expansion in Asia Minor and along the North African coast. These events caused important changes in its defensive organization. After the attempts to recover lost territories had failed, the empire was forced to limit itself to its new borders. The main mass of imperial territories lay, henceforth, in western and central Asia Minor along with Thrace and a part of the Aegean coasts. The situation was so critical that Emperor Constans II (641 AD – 668 AD) attempted to transfer the empire's seat to Syracuse in Sicily. He remained in Italy from 663 AD until his assassination in 668 AD, when Constantinople became the seat of government once more. His death thus brought to a close the final attempt to return the empire's core back to Italy.

The Italian regions that remained under the control of the empire in the late 7th century came under the Exarchate of Ravenna, which covered the coast of the northern part of the Adriatic Sea, the towns of Latio and Campania, Calabria and the islands of Sicily, Sardinia, and Corsica. The Exarchate of Carthage in North Africa survived until the late 7th century, when the Arabs occupied it. In 700 AD, the empire actually consisted of Asia Minor, some coastal regions of the Aegean, Italy, and the islands of the eastern and central Mediterranean. Almost all the provinces that had remained under Byzantine control were Greek-speaking, a fact that led to the complete Hellenization of the Eastern Roman Empire.

The empire's military forces were assembled in the limited geographical area of the remaining territories and their reorganization began. In the following centuries, two categories of military units were developed, the army of the "themes" that were created in the provinces and the army of the *tagmata*, consisting of more mobile units of mainly mercenaries that were initially found in the capital but were later also located in other large towns. This change took place slowly and progressively, spanning, in fact, the period from the late 7th

(Opposite page) Illustration showing an Emperor accompanied by his bodyguards. (Illuminated manuscript from John Skylitzes' chronicle, National Library, Madrid)

λοχοί ωΤοισεγαψΤιοις · καιΤωσαιφηΔικωκαταπωηξαμψοι · ωολιωΜεραωγαφοροψ
πωψηκωρ · ηραωδεκαιΤωσκλασιωπψρωωολω ωΤπυρι ·
ωλεερωωωψ πψρπολ   ΤΗΤωΝΕΗΑΗΤφλοΝ ·

Representation of the use of "Greek fire" during a sea battle. (Illuminated manuscript from John Skylitzes' chronicle, National Library, Madrid)

century until the 10th, beginning with the reorganization of the empire's eastern forces around the late 7th century. The military units that were under the commands of the old *Magistri Militum* remained united, but they were now called by the Greek term *themata* ("themes") and were transferred to other regions. The armies of the two Magistri *Militum Praesentales* remained in the regions of northwestern Asia Minor and Eastern Thrace, covering, however, a smaller area of territory than in the previous centuries and were now called the "Opsikion theme." The forces of the *Magister Militum per Orientem*, that were already termed the "Anatolikon theme" (theme of the army of the East), settled in the southern part of central Asia Minor. The army of the *Magister Militum per Armeniam*, which was, henceforth, called the "Armeniakon theme" (theme of the army of Armenia), covered the northern and eastern provinces of Asia Minor. The forces of the *Magister Militum per Thracias*, called the "Thrakesion theme" (theme of the army of Thrace), having been stationed in Egypt for some time and failing to save this province from the Arab onslaught, settled in the fertile provinces of western central Asia Minor. Eventually, these units gave their name to the provinces where they settled, and the term "theme" ended up meaning not only the military unit but also the administrative division in which it settled. In Europe, the largest part of the Balkan provinces had been lost to Slav and Avar raids. The empire retained under its control very few places along the coastline, and these were incorporated into the maritime "theme" of Carabisiani, the center of which was initially the island of Rhodes in the southeastern Aegean.

The "themes" constituted military and political administrations. The general commanding the military forces of each "theme" also monitored the judicial and tax services of his region of jurisdiction. The borders of the "themes" did not remain stable, and the general tendency prevailing over the following decades and centuries was for them to be split into smaller areas, whereas smaller in area "themes" were created in those regions that were taken by the empire's enemies in the late 10th and early 11th centuries. This practice emerged due to internal reasons, as it decreased the possibility of a theme's governor rising against the central power and claiming the imperial throne. Thus, from four initial "themes" in Asia Minor, the empire was divided into 13 themes in the 7th century and a total of 40 themes by the 11th century. However, in the second half of the 10th century, the small frontier "themes" of Asia Minor were united under larger

Representation of Saracen ships. The Saracens, with their pirate raids, forced the Empire into a tight corner until Crete was re-occupied by Nikephoros Phocas, which then served as a base. (Illuminated manuscript from John Skylitzes' chronicle, National Library, Madrid)

administrations monitored by a dignitary titled *Dux* or *Katepano*. The foundation of the "themes" was combined with a new structure in the organization of the Byzantine army. The soldiers serving in the army of each "theme" were allocated plots of land, which they farmed and exploited, in return for their military services. There was thus created a class of soldier/farmers, whose actual duty was to defend the empire in the following centuries (from the 8th to the 10th), until the recovery of lost Asia Minor territories with the use of *tagmatic* units.

The forces that settled in the various frontier regions were integrated into the local societies and, to a large extent, lost the mentality and flexibility of the old *Comitatenses*. These soldiers constituted a kind of military aristocracy, who were valued in their regions but, over time, proved particularly covetous in defending their privileges. Apart from these standing professional soldiers, local militias were formed in the frontier regions, being activated in times of increased hostile activity. During the late 8th century, the "themes" were reinforced with the formation of a number of special divisions, named *kleisourarchiai*, for the purpose of safeguarding the borders. The mission of these contingents was to maintain watch over points of strategic importance, especially the passes *(kleisourai)* habitually used by invaders. A local military aristocracy was formed in these regions, constructing their own fortresses, living off revenue from fighting the Arabs and maintaining a relative autonomy from the central administration in Constantinople. These were the so-called *akrites* (from the Greek word *akrai*, meaning "fringes", "borders") whose exploits lived on as legends in the collective memory of the population they protected, even up to the modern Greece. This march of events proves that the central administration in Constantinople had granted a larger autonomy to the local frontier guards, so that they would then face the constant threats of invasion more efficiently.

Similar changes also took place in the coastal regions of the Aegean and southwest Asia Minor, where three maritime "themes" were formed in the early 9th century. The Arabs had already turned into fearsome pirates and the empire's coastal areas were at the mercy of their raids. To confront them it was often required to mobilize powerful naval as well as land forces. The empire gradually lost many of its naval bases in the Mediterranean, including those on the Balearic Islands, Sicily, and Crete, in the first half of the 9th century. The Balearic Islands and even more so, Crete, became especially important bases for the piratical activities of the Saracens (Arab pirates), who began their depredations in Spain, gradually expanding across the entire Mediterranean.

Deterring the Arabs and Iconoclasm

Having deprived the empire of the largest portion of its southern provinces, the Arabs attempted to occupy Constantinople itself. Their first effort took place in 673 AD – 678 AD, when the forces of Caliph Mu'awiyah blockaded the city's outlet to the sea. This extended siege, however, failed to pose a serious threat to the empire's capital, as the besiegers ceased operations during the winter and withdrew. The city's most severe ordeal occurred in 717 AD – 718 AD, when an Arab fleet under General Maslamah blockaded Constantinople from the sea and disembarked an army on the coast with the aim of attacking its landward fortifications. The city was finally saved thanks to a combination of "Greek fire," the harsh winter that exhausted the besiegers, an unexpected Bulgarian attack on the Arabs, and the leadership of Leon III the Isaurian (717 AD – 741 AD).

The Bulgarians had already risen to prominence as the most powerful barbarians in the Balkans. Their attack on the Arabs was not to help Constantinople, but because they wanted to occupy it themselves. In the succeeding centuries, until their final subjugation by Basil II the *Boulgaroktonos* (actually meaning "Bulgar-Slayer") in the early 11th century, the Bulgarians constituted one of the empire's most persistent enemies. Their attacks prevented the development of the Balkan provinces. Macedonia and Thrace were particularly threatened by their presence and imperial control over them was inconsistent, with the exception of the large fortified towns, such as Thessalonica and Adrianople. The consequences of the Bulgarian presence were magnified by the expansion of the Slavic peoples in the western part of the Balkans all the way to the Peloponnesus. A large part of the hellenic peninsula was outside the control of the empire, which only retained the fortified towns. Chaos prevailed in the countryside as Slav groups, who formed their own communities called *sklavinies*, had occupied and settled in large areas.

Illustration showing the launch of "Greek fire" from a siege tower using a handheld device (cheirosiphon). (Vatican Library)

The "Greek fire" (in Greek *hygron pyr*, meaning "liquid fire") that helped save Constantinople in 717 AD – 718 AD was a flammable mixture, the composition of which was one of the empire's most closely guarded secrets. The use of a similar formula had already been known since the 6th century, when the imperial army used a mixture of sulphur, tar oil and naphtha during Justinian's wars. This mixture may have used extra nitre, that caused a rapid combustion or explosion, in combination with other materials such as sulphur, resin, colophony or oil. This lethal weapon was later improved by Callinicus, a Greek engineer from Heliopolis in Syria (today's Baalbek in Lebanon), although his improvements remain unknown to this day. It is likely that the improvements were not with the composition of the mixture but with the manufacturing of the delivery mechanism -a *siphon*. It appears that,

The occupation and sack of Thessalonica by the Arabs in 904 AD was one of the most catastrophic events in the history of the empire. (Illuminated manuscript from John Skylitzes' chronicle, National Library, Madrid)

until Callinicus' time, this flammable mixture was used against the enemy in special vessels but later the discharge took place from special siphons. Until the 9th century, "Greek fire" was only used in boats and in the fortification towers, as its projection required bulky siphons. From the late 9th century, a portable projection device (*cheirosiphon* meaning "hand operated pipe") began to be used, which could be transported and operated by a single operator.

While the contribution of Leon III Isaurian is deemed important in regard to confronting the Arabian besiegers of Constantinople in 717 AD – 718 AD, he was also the emperor who later launched a number of expeditions that halted the advance of the Arabs and ensured the maintenance of the power of the empire in central and western Asia Minor. The work of Leon III continued under his son, Constantine V (741 AD – 775 AD), who successfully faced not only the Arabs but also the Bulgarians. The names of these two emperors are also connected with one of the most serious crises in the interior of the empire. They tried to prevent the adoration of religious icons (a policy that was called "Iconoclasm") and to impose restrictions on the operation of monasteries that had expanded disproportionately, had acquired large fortunes, and were depriving the state of precious income due to the tax exemptions they enjoyed. In a number of cases, the monasteries allied themselves with the large landowners, who were also called *dynatoi* (meaning "potent"), and tried to expand their power by undermining the central imperial authority. These landowners had acquired extensive swathes of land, much wealth and, in many cases, offered fortified mansions and groups of mercenaries to their service. They tried to expand their land even further by pressing minor landowners into selling their properties. Even soldiers of the "thematic" army, who possessed areas of land for their own maintenance, failed to escape the pressure of the "potent."

Iconoclasm was clearly not merely a religious matter but had profound political implications. The supporters of the icons reacted to the imperial policy with obstinacy and often with fanaticism. Behind the faithful and often unsophisticated, pious Iconophiles (supporters of the adoration of the icons) hid the clandestine agents, such as the monasteries and the powerful landowners who wished only to protect their privileges. Iconoclasm caused problems for the empire for decades. The first, most intense phase lasted from 726 AD until 787 AD, whereas the second phase, which was milder, lasted from 815 AD until 843 AD. A consequence of Iconoclasm was the division of the empire's "themes" into

Iconophiles and Iconoclasts, which undermined the unity of the state in a difficult period, while it was under threat from all sides. It was also the root cause of many of the problems in the emperor's relations with the Pope.

The empire between East and West

The Popes considered Rome as part of the empire until the 8th century. In reality, however, the weakened Byzantine state was unable to protect the Pope and his city, which was threatened by the Lombards. Taking advantage of the fact that the emperor had turned his attention towards the salvation of Asia Minor and what remained of the Balkans, in 751 AD, the Lombards occupied Ravenna, the West's old imperial capital and the most important center of Byzantine power in northern Italy. Henceforth, Byzantine power was limited to the southern regions of Calabria, Apulia (modern Italian Puglia) and the islands of Sicily and Sardinia. Thus, the Pope was forced to seek support from the Franks, the most powerful of the barbarian tribes that had settled in Gaul on the ruins of the Roman Empire.

The Frankish kings agreed to help the Pope, provided he acknowledged them in return. Their collaboration reached its peak in 800 AD, when the primate of the western Church crowned Charlemagne in Rome, as sovereign of the Franks and Roman Emperor. This action constituted an open challenge to the Byzantines of the Eastern Roman Empire of Constantinople, which considered their state to be the sole holder of the Imperial Roman title. To the Byzantines, Charlemagne was nothing more than a ridiculous barbarian, who usurped a title whose importance and sanctity he could not understand. But in reality Charlemagne was the West's most powerful monarch and his coronation created a fundamental problem for the empire. The West actually disavowed the primacy of the Eastern Empire and claimed its own independence from the formal political suzerainty and the religious guidance of the East. The notion of the Western Roman Empire was firmly founded in the Western conscience and the Byzantine Empire had to come to terms with this. But, for the Byzantines, only their own emperor was the keeper of Roman tradition and power, and this conviction lasted until the final fall of the empire in 1453 AD.

The period between the 7th and the mid-9th centuries was characterized by the empire's efforts to defend itself, and to deter the Arab attacks in the east and along the Aegean coast, and Bulgarians in the west. In the following decades, however, from the mid-9th until the early 10th centuries, the empire assumed an aggressive initiative and reoccupied a large part of the territories that had been lost to the Arabs, while it completely subjugated the Bulgarian state, thus restoring the old Roman border along the southern bank of the Danube. In the east, the empire's frontiers were expanded to Mount Ararat in Armenia and northern Mesopotamia. Byzantine sovereignty was restored in the strategic islands of the Eastern Mediterranean, Crete, Cyprus, and Rhodes, as well as in the southern part of Italy, in Calabria, and Apulia. This period was called "the Byzantine epopee (saga)" and was the most brilliant time in the course of the empire's middle period. During that time, gifted military leaders ascended the imperial throne, such as Nikephoros II

Gold coin showing Emperor Isaac I Komnenos in military dress. (Monetary Museum, Athens)

Phocas (963 AD – 969 AD), John I Tzimiskes (969 AD – 976 AD) and primarily Basil II the Boulgaroktonos (963 AD – 1025 AD), although he actually began to exercise power in 976 AD. The military successes during this period were mainly due to the *tagmata*, the elite divisions of the Byzantine army that had been created using the imperial guard in Constantinople as the nucleus. On the other hand, the "thematic" army functioned more as a supporting force and was progressively marginalized and weakened.

To protect its borders, however, the Byzantine Empire did not limit itself to military actions but also developed robust diplomatic activity. The aim of Byzantine diplomacy was to ensure the friendship of chosen neighboring barbarian tribes. By these efforts, the tribes were convinced to halt their raids against the empire, or turned into a source of valuable mercenaries. The fundamental axis for the management of good relations with a barbarian population was their proselytism to the Christian Orthodox religion. The greatest success of this policy was the christianization of the Bulgarians and the Russians in the 9th and 10th centuries respectively. At first, the Bulgarians continued to threaten the empire, but eventually both peoples turned out to be adherents of Byzantine culture. Indeed, the Russians offered military assistance to Emperor Basil II (later named the *Boulgaroktonos*) during the first years of his reign, when he was confronted by a revolt of a number of powerful landowners in Asia Minor.

The successes of the Byzantine epopee produced an overly complacent attitude towards security in Constantinople. The central imperial government considered the state to be invulnerable to its neighbors and if an invading army dared to cross the imperial borders they would immediately be faced by the formidable imperial military forces, without having the chance to cause any depredation in the interior, the frontier regions not being considered of equal significance. This feeling of security was also supported by the awe in which its neighbors held the empire over a number of decades, since no intruder dared cross its borders after Bulgaria's subjugation in 1018 AD, until the advent of the Seljuk Turks in the mid-11th century. As a result of this mentality, the army, particularly the "thematic" one, was neglected. The powerful landowners gained ground by exploiting the progressive disintegration of the "thematic" army in order to increase their wealth by occupying military land. Emperor Basil II, the Bulgar Slayer, sought to prevent this by enacting corresponding laws, but

Armed conflict between the imperial army and the military forces of a pretender. Battles such as these for the imperial throne were one of the main causes behind the weakening of the empire. (Illuminated manuscript from Constantine Manasses' chronicle, Apostolical Library, Vatican)

The occupation of a city by the imperial army. (Illuminated manuscript from John Skylitzes' chronicle, National Library, Madrid)

following his death, these were either abolished or fell into disuse. At the same time, the *tagmata* units turned largely into mercenary ones, as most of the empire's "themes" could not, or did not wish to serve in them. The empire was wealthy and was able to afford thousands of mercenaries, to whom it entrusted its fate, since the purely Byzantine units, constituted by its "themes," continuously decreased in number and prestige.

The result of these changes was that the empire turned into a "colossus with feet of clay" by the mid-11th century. Externally, it still appeared powerful but, in reality, its borders would collapse if enough pressure were applied. This pressure was actually applied by two new opponents of the empire, the Normans in the West and the Seljuk Turks in the East, a powerful intruder who had already come to prevail in the regions of Mesopotamia and Iran by that time. Some of their units spread out to the empire's Eastern borders while small, mounted parties began raiding in Asia Minor. Emperor Romanos IV Diogenis (1068 AD – 1071 AD) attempted to confront them by organizing an expedition to the empire's Eastern borders. His army fought the Seljuk Turks at Manzikert in 1071 AD, where it was defeated and the emperor captured.

For the first time in the empire's history, a Byzantine emperor had been captured in battle. Following his defeat, Romanos IV Diogenis was overthrown, but his successors also failed to prevent Seljuk expansion into Asia Minor. By 1081 AD, just ten years after Manzikert, the Seljuks had occupied the largest part of Asia Minor, apart from a few places along the Black Sea coast and the Bosporus. Also in 1071 AD, the year of the Manzikert disaster, the empire lost its last fortress in Italy when the Normans occupied the town of Baris (modern Bari). More than five centuries of Byzantine sovereignty in southern Italy were thus terminated, a period that had begun with the reoccupation of the region by Justinian. The overly optimistic view of the empire's security and indifference to the defense of the borders that prevailed in Constantinople during the previous decades had cost the empire dear.

The Komnenian dynasty and the Crusades

The loss of Asia Minor and the obvious inability of the empire to recover its lost territories forced the Emperor Alexios I Komnenos (1081 AD – 1118 AD) to

FOOT SOLDIER OF THE BYZANTINE ARMY (MIDDLE 10th CENTURY AD)
This particular illustration is based on the uniform research and reconstruction carried out by Professor Timothy Dawson and the military manuals written by Emperor Nikephoros Phokas. Instead of a metal helmet, the soldier wears a turban made of either linen or cotton fabric wrapped around a cylindrical hat made of soft material. This cheap helmet substitute absorbed the dynamic energy of sword blows to the forehead. The soldier's body is protected by a thick padded zava *with detachable sleeves. On his feet he wears leather mid-calf boots (*mouzakia *in Byzantine terminology), and carries a battleaxe (*tzikourion*), a double-edged sword (*spathion*) -not visible in the illustration- and a kite-shaped shield (*scutari*). (uniform reconstruction and illustration by Christos Giannopoulos, based on Timothy Dawson's published conclusions and research)*

request the Pope's assistance, although relations between the two Churches, the Eastern Orthodox and the Western Catholic one, had been in crisis since 1054 AD. The Emperor requested the Pope to send western mercenaries to Constantinople to assist in the recovery of Asia Minor. However, Pope Urban II announced the organization of a Crusade to the East instead of sending mercenaries. According to the Pope's concept, any western European inhabitant could participate in the expedition for the liberation of Jerusalem and the Holy Land, where Jesus had lived. This call was effective and a large number of knights along with peasants and urban riffraff set off for Jerusalem, with Constantinople as an intermediary stop. This march of events was not what Alexios I Komnenos asked nor really wished for, but the Emperor managed to exploit the dynamics of the events. He convinced the leaders of the Crusade to pledge their allegiance to him and to yield to him any Asia Minor territories they could occupy. In this way, the empire recovered a large part of the western coastal regions of Asia Minor. During the succeeding years, Alexios I Komnenos and his successor John II (1118 AD – 1143 AD) also managed to occupy the southern coasts of Asia Minor and to contain the Seljuk Turks in the interior. The son and successor of John II, Manuel I Komnenos (1143 AD – 1180 AD), tried to carry on their work but was defeated by the Seljuks at the Battle of Myriokephalon in 1176 AD. Following this defeat, he was compelled to grant the victors the fortresses that protected western Asia Minor from their raids. The Seljuks took advantage of the situation and, within a few decades, had managed to occupy a major part of the region, limiting the Byzantines to the northern and northwestern areas of Asia Minor.

The Normans also constituted a threat that was equally dangerous to the Seljuks. After completing the conquest of southern Italy and Sicily, they considered they were powerful enough to strike at the very heart of the empire by mounting raids in the Balkan and Aegean regions. Their aim was to plunder the wealth of the empire (should they succeed), and to occupy Constantinople, in order to create a great Norman state in the East, in southern Italy and the Balkans. The empire was subjected to several Norman raids in 1081 AD – 1085 AD, in 1107 AD, in 1147 AD – 1149 AD and in 1185 AD, the third and fourth raids being the most devastating; during the third, the silk industries of Corinth and Thebes were destroyed, causing great damage to the empire's economy, while, during the fourth raid, Thessalonica, the empire's second important city, was occupied and ruthlessly plundered. The fall of Thessalonica was the reason behind the overthrow of the last emperor of the Komnenos family, Andronikos I (1183 AD – 1185 AD).

In 1185 AD, the Angeloi ascended to the throne; a new dynasty that was eventually to lead the empire into terminal decline. While the Seljuks expanded in the east, in the Balkans the Bulgarians and the Serbs managed to break away from imperial control. Moreover, the Angeloi were divided because of a dynastic dispute. Emperor Isaac II Angelos (1185 AD – 1195 AD) was overthrown by his brother, Alexios III Angelos, who exploited the people's dissatisfaction with Isaac's misrule and the empire's territorial contraction. Alexios III Angelos, however, proved less capable than his predecessor and certainly his inferior. In 1201 AD, Alexios IV, son of Isaac II, till then a hostage in Constantinople with his father, managed to escape and flee to the West, where he requested assistance in regaining his throne. At that time, the Fourth Crusade was being organized, the leaders of which heard the proposals of young Alexios with interest and were induced to help in return for an important pecuniary sum and the subjugation of the Eastern Church to the West.

The Crusaders arrived in Constantinople in 1203 AD and restored Alexios and his father to the throne. But when they realized that the emperor was not in a position to fulfill his promises, as he had neither sufficient military forces to defend the imperial territories or wealth to pay them, they became belligerent. The Crusaders' provocative behavior enraged the inhabitants of Constantinople, who restored Alexios IV and Isaac II to the throne. This turn of events gave the Crusaders the excuse to attack and occupy Constantinople in April 1204 AD. This event signaled the end of an era. The Eastern Roman Empire, which had managed to repulse the deadly threats of hordes of barbarians from 395 AD until 1204 AD, collapsed under the blows from the Christians of the West. The Byzantine Empire managed to partly heal its wounds and survive for another two and half centuries, but it would never regain the prestige and greatness that characterized it before the Fourth Crusade.

The organization of the Byzantine army from the 7th to the 12th centuries

The frontier region

The loss of most of the imperial provinces to the Arabs, and the continual incursions of the Arabs as well as the Bulgarians in the remaining territories of the empire, brought about the definitive abandonment of the old "linear" Roman perception for the protection of the borders. The imperial army no longer camped along the borders, while all the major cities were henceforth heavily fortified. In the event of an invasion, the imperial forces attempted to meet the enemy in open battle, but only if there was a high probability of success, although they usually preferred to counteract their enemies by ambushes and ongoing expeditions of harassment. In 779 AD, Emperor Leon IV (775 AD – 780 AD) ordered every general in Asia Minor to assemble 3,000 elite soldiers and to adopt harassment tactics against the Arab army that had advanced deep into the western department of central Asia Minor, all the way to Dorylaion. Because of these tactics, the Arabs dared not divide their forces into small units and they extended their raids throughout all the Asia Minor provinces. The emperor had also ordered the destruction of all supplies found outside the fortified cities. In this way, 15 days later the Arabs were forced to withdraw, but they had already managed to reach the heart of Asia Minor, fully coordinated and never called to battle by the imperial army.

The application of regular, continual harassment and the avoidance of a large set-piece battle resulted in the intruders not being driven back before they encroached onto imperial territory, while the frontier regions suffered continuous pillaging, with resulting highly detrimental consequences for the economy of the Byzantine state and the morale of its people. In a number of cases, even small

CHERSON

DALMATIA

PAPHLAGONIA   ARMENIAKON

DYRRACHION   STRYMON   THRAKE
                                        Constantinople   CHALDIA
                          MAKEDONIA   •
                                                                          KOLONEIA
THESSALONIKI   OPSIKION   BOUKELLARION   MESO-
LAGOBARDIA   CHARSIANON   POTAMIA
         NIKOPOLIS   SEBASTEIA

                          HELLAS   ANATOLIKON
KEFALLENIA   THRAKESION   KAPPADOKIA
         PELOPONESSOS   LYKANDOS

                          KIBYRAIOTON   SELEUKIA

*The Byzantine "themes"
during the 10th century.
The development of the
"themes" is attributed
to Heraclius' policy at
the time of the two-front
struggle against
the Persians and Avars
and constituted
its most diacritical
accomplishment.*

groups of invaders managed to attack, plunder and withdraw beyond the borders before the imperial army had time to respond. There was thus created a kind of a no-man's-land between the empire and its neighbors, especially along the Eastern borders – a region not under the total control of either side. Its inhabitants, however, remained and continued to work. These people lived in semi-autonomous communities and collaborated with both sides. Among them were Christians who, officially, depended on the empire but only to the degree that its power could be imposed on them, and their loyalty was doubtful.

Along the empire's Balkan borders the situation was much the same. It was at this point that the "themes" were developed, being organized like those in Asia Minor. The most potent threat to imperial power in the Balkans were, henceforth, the Bulgarians, a Mongol people that had intermixed with the Slav groups situated between the Danube and the Aimos mountain range. The Bulgarian raids were frequent and brutal and, because of their effect, quite often the empire lost control of the Macedonian and Thracian territories that lay outside the heavily fortified cities. Throughout the conflict against the Bulgarians there were also some agreed periods of peace, but despite these agreements small groups of invaders were always active. As a result, some fortified Byzantine settlements, which were isolated in regions controlled by Bulgarians or Slavs, were in a situation of permanent martial readiness. In these regions, to a large extent the two opponents applied the policy of military colonization. Groups of people from other regions were forced or convinced that it was in their best interests to move to the frontier line in order to contribute to its defense. The empire primarily moved peoples from central and Eastern Asia Minor, while the Bulgarians used Slav groups for this purpose.

OFFICER OF THE IMPERIAL EXCUBITORES **BODYGUARD (870 AD)**
The armourers of the Byzantine army's elite units combined
Turco-Islamic elements with the older Roman styles.
The bodyguard illustrated here wears a feathered
Turanic helmet over a mail coif while a cuirass, that is
a combination of both mail and lamellar plates, protects
his upper body. He carries a decorated round shield and, for
offense, uses a double-edged sword (paramerion)
and a spiked battleaxe (tzikourion) *that is probably*
a variant of the older Germanic fransisca. *The white*
garment worn over the lamellar klibanion *probably*
denotes some particular Excubitores *unit.*
(illustration by Christos Giannopoulos)

The "thematic" army in the middle period

In the 6th and 7th centuries, the process of Hellenizing the imperial army by replacing all Latin terms with Greek or Hellenized ones was completed. Also contributing to this process were the more general changes in the borders and the defensive structure of the Eastern Roman Empire that led to an in-depth reorganization of its army. The title *Magister Militum* was replaced with that of *Strategos* ("general") with each general commanding a military unit ("theme"), in charge of the region where it was located. Two exceptions were the "Opsikion theme," whose commander was a *Komes*, and the "Optimatoi theme," commanded by a *Domesticos*. During the reign of Leon VI the Wise (886 AD – 912 AD), the most powerful "theme" could field 15,000 troops, while the smallest 4,000. These forces were made up of soldiers that lived mainly by farming their own land, situated in the region where they served. Each commander of a "theme" had his personal guard, constituting by a *spatharios*. These were divided in *ekatontarchiai* ("centuries") commanded by *Kentarchoi* or *spatharioi*. Three officials, *Protonotarios*, *Praetor* and *Chartoularios* assisted the commander of the "theme" with his administrative duties. A *Protonotarios* was the person in charge of financial management and reported to the *Logothesion tou Genikou* ("logothesion" was the term used at the time by the Byzantines for "ministry") who controlled the logistics, soldiers' salaries, and the collection of the necessary supplies, if and when the imperial army passed through his jurisdiction. A *Praetor* was in charge of law enforcement and controlled the administration; the *Chartoularios* was responsible for taxation and public revenue. In the 8th and 9th centuries, the Byzantines also used the titles of *Dux* or *Katepano*, meaning the governor of an independent force, which usually undertook a specific mission and did not come under the local administrations of the territories they passed through.

Each theme was divided into *tourmai* or *mere* ("divisions") composed of *moirai* ("parts"). Each *tourma* (a word stemming from the Latin term "turma," which initially meant "crowd of people") was under the administration of a *Tourmarches*. A *Tourmarches* had a specific position in the hierarchy, proportional to that of the senior generals, and exercised both military and political power. Each *Tourmarches* in the frontier "themes" usually had his own seat in a fortified city. In each "theme" there was also a *Tourmarches*, who served on the general's staff and was considered to be relatively junior to the rest of the *Tourmarchai* who autonomously administered some parts of the "theme." The *Tourmarchai* were divided into two categories, the superior (*prokritoteroi*) and the junior (*elattoteroi*). The *tourmai* were usually divided into three *moirai* or *droungoi*, each *droungos* corresponding roughly to a *chiliarchia* and commanded by a *Droungarios* or *Moirarchos*. A *droungos* was divided into *banda*, units of roughly 200 soldiers. Each *droungos* usually had two to five *banda*.

ORDER OF BATTLE OF A CAVALRY *DEKARCHIA*		
1st line	Dekarchos	Pentarchos
2nd line	Spearman	Spearman
3rd line	Archer	Archer
4th line	Archer	Archer
5th line	Tetrarchos	Ouragos

THE ORGANISATION OF THE MILITARY UNITS OF THE BYZANTINE ARMY AND ITS HIERARCHY DURING THE MIDDLE BYZANTINE PERIOD (9th CENTURY AD)					
Thema (Theme)			Strategos (General)		
Tourma or Meros			Tourmarches or Merarchos		
Droungos or Moira			Droungarios or Moirarchos		
Bandon			Komes		
Infantry units	Allaghion	Ekatontarchos or Kentarchos (Centurion, commander in two Allaghia)	Cavalry units	Allaghion	Pente-kontarches
	Lochagia	Lochagos			
		Dekarchos			Dekarchos
		Pentarchos			Pentarchos
		Tetrarchos			Tetrarchos
		Ouragos			Ouragos

Each *bandon* had its own banner. A *Komes* was the commander of a *bandon*, both infantry and cavalry units. In each infantry *bandon* there were 16 *lochagiai*, with 16 soldiers in each and a *Lochagos* in command. The junior officers in each *lochagia* were a *Dekarchos*, a *Pentarchos*, a *Tetrarchos,* and an *Ouragos* (meaning "file closer"). Four *lochagiai* constituted an *allaghion*, whereas a *Centurion* (*Ekatontarchos* or *Kentarchos* commanded every two *allaghia*. In heavy infantry units, three quarters of the soldiers were spearmen, called *skoutatoi*, while the rest were archers. The archers constituted a *lochagia* in each *allaghion* of *skoutatoi* or formed a separate *allaghion*. In the units of light infantry there was a distinction between spearmen and archers. Sometimes in the light infantry *banda*, a *lochagia* was composed of 8 instead of 16 soldiers. The cavalry *banda* were divided into three *ekatontarchies*, each one under the command of a *Kentarchos*. The senior *Kentarchos* was also deputy commander of the *bandon* and held the rank of *Ilarchos*. In the late 9th century, the *ekatontarchies* of cavalry were abolished and replaced by six *allaghia*, each comprising 50 horsemen and, most probably, commanded by officers called *Pentekontarchai*. In the cavalry there were also the junior ranks of a *Dekarchos*, a *Pentarchos*, a *Tetrarchos,* and an *Ouragos* ("file closer"), while the units consisted of a combination of lancers and archers, but the rank-holders were always spearmen. In battle, a *dekarchia* of cavalry deployed in five ranks of two troopers. In the first rank there was a *Dekarchos* and a *Pentarchos*. Behind them was a rank with two lancers, then two ranks with four archers and, in the last rank, there was a *Tetrarchos* and an *Ouragos*. Theoretically each *bandon* of heavy infantry had 256 soldiers, while each bandon of cavalry comprised 300 horsemen, but in practice these numbers were lower. Moreover, contemporary sources reveal that the terms *bandon* and *tourma* often appeared to refer to units of different sizes, an element proving that there were many differentiations in this organization.

The hierarchy of the Byzantine army was changed during the period of recovery of the territories lost to the Arabs and Bulgarians. The army's senior commander was the general of the Anatolic theme. Two *domestikoi* were under his orders, the "Domestikos of the Scholae of the East" (for the Asiatic provinces) and the "Domestikos of the Scholae of the West" (for the European provinces). The *domestikoi* were formally upgraded with the addition of an honorary adjective to their title and were henceforth called *Megaloi* (Grand) *Domestikoi*. The *domestikoi* assisted the two corresponding *Stratopedarchaes* ("Masters of the Camp") with their duties, one for the East and the other for the West. Two "Domestikoi of Excubitors" followed in the hierarchy and subordinate to these were two *Topoteretaes* of the *Scholae*.

During the reign of Nikephoros Phocas (963 AD – 969 AD) the number of personnel in the older units decreased and new ones appeared in their place. For the first time, terms like *taxiarchia* ("large army unit") and *Taxiarches* (the commanding officer of a *taxiarchia*) appeared, mainly referring to infantry units. A brigade was a unit corresponding in force with that of a *chiliarchia* and consisted of 500 spearmen, 200 *kontaratoi* (armed with spears) and 300 archers. A *chiliarchia*, based on the former army organization, corresponded to a *droungos*, but by that time 1,000 soldiers made up the force of a *tourma*. Because of the reduction of its force, a *droungos* was identical to a *bandon* and the ranks of *Droungarios* and *Komes* were amalgamated. The appearance of the *Drungarokometas* ("droungarios-komes") rank is proof of this development. In the organization of cavalry, the term *parataxis* appeared, consisting of 10 banda of 50 soldiers. Simultaneously, the titles of *Archegetes* and *Hoplitarches* appeared, referring to commanders of large units mainly consisting of infantry forces. A *Hoplitarches* was superior to a *Taxiarches*, while the rank of *Archegetes* reportedly corresponded to that of *Hoplitarches*, or commander of all military forces. The ranks of *Stratopedarches* and *Ethnarches* also appeared. *Ethnarches* was a title possibly used for dignitaries that commanded *ethne* (units of foreign mercenaries, "ethne" is the Greek word for "nations"). Other ranks that existed in former times were vested with increased prestige and greater power. In the 9th century, a *Protostrator* was the head of the emperor's mounted entourage. In the 11th century, the *Protostratores* rose to be vice governors of the imperial army, subordinate in the hierarchy to the *Domestikoi* of the East and West.

The *tagmata* and the Varangians

The *tagmata* were created during the reign of Constantine V (741 AD – 775 AD) and they constituted the solid nucleus of the Byzantine army and were initially identified with the imperial guard that was stationed in Constantinople. Each had a limited number of troops that were, however, better paid and constituted a highly trained cadre during expeditions. Eventually the *tagmata* evolved into mobile forces under the control of the central administration, somewhat similar to the old *Comitatenses*, and were mainly composed of mercenaries, foreigners to a large degree, whose standard of discipline and loyalty was proportional to their salary. Although the initial seat of the *tagmata* was Constantinople, its units were later also stationed in other major cities of the empire. The *tagmata* mainly consisted of four units of cavalry: the *Scholae*, *Arithmoi* ("Numbers"), *Excubitors* and *Hikanatoi* (meaning "Worthies"). The term *tagmata* could, however, also cover other units, such as the *Hetaireia* (meaning in Greek "company"). The *Scholae* were the oldest of these bodies and, in some instances, the term *scholarioi* referred to all soldiers of the *tagmata* and not only those of the *Scholae*. During the 9th century, 6,000 soldiers and another 6,000 auxiliaries served in the *tagmata*. A *Domestikos*, with the exception of the *Arithmoi*, which was commanded

MERCENARY BODYGUARD - MEMBER OF THE VARANGIAN GUARD (1000 AD - 1050 AD)
This particular warrior is one of the many Slavic-Scandinavian or Saxon mercenaries who took an oath to protect the Byzantine emperors with their lives, generation after generation. His primary offensive weapon, native to his area of origin, is the large Scandinavian battleaxe, an ideal weapon for inflicting grievous damage to both men and horses. Secondary offensive weapons consisted of a large seax knife and the Scandinavian broadsword (partly visible in the illustration). For his defense he wears a chain mail coat, a round shield decorated with pagan motifs, a Turco-Scandinavian-style helmet with nasal bar and, finally, the segmented arm and knee guards. (uniform research and reconstruction by Christos Giannopoulos)

*Illustration of
a floating siege tower.
(Vatican Library)*

by a *Droungarios*, commanded each of the four *tagmata* units. The senior of all these was the "Domestikos of the Scholae." Later, this rank, and the corresponding administration, was divided between the ranks of "Domestikos of the Schools of the East" (for the Asiatic provinces) and "Domestikos of the Schools of the West" (for the European provinces). The vice governor of each unit was a *Topoteretes*. The role of the *tagmata* became more important during the 9th century, when the Byzantines set out to recover the empire's lost territories from the Arabs and Bulgarians. It was, at this time, that the *tagmata* proved to be the imperial army's pre-eminent strike force.

The formation of the *tagmata* was a manifestation of the empire's general tendency to rely on mercenary groups, comprised of nationals or foreigners. These mercenaries were inducted into elite units and were used for a specific expedition or a campaign or undertook permanent guard duties. During the period following the Byzantine epopee, that is, the second half of the 11th century, the *tagmata* became neglected and were eventually dissolved. During the reign of Alexios I Komnenos only two similar units existed as the emperor's guards, the *Excubitors* and the *Athanatoi* ("Immortals"). After the death of Alexios I these too were dissolved and the emperor's security was assigned mainly to the Varangian Guard.

The Varangian Guard is probably the best-known mercenary unit of the Byzantine army. The word "Varangian," by which, initially, the Russians and later the Byzantines called the Scandinavians, probable stems from the ancient Norwegian word *var*, meaning "commitment" from which stems *varjasy* "mercenary". It initially referred to a group of people that had sworn faith to each other and obedience to certain common rules, having agreed on the distribution of profits resulting from their activities. In some cases, during the 10th century, the empire used mercenaries from Russia, where many Scandinavians from Sweden had settled. In 988 AD, Vladimir of Kiev sent to Constantinople a *druzhina*, that is 6,000 men, under orders to serve Emperor Basil II the Boulgaroktonos (976 AD – 1025 AD). The emperor was so impressed with these warriors that he decided to use them as his personal guard. The nucleus of that select body of mercenaries was thus formed, in which other young men from Scandinavia were also recruited. Even warriors from noble families, such as Harald Hardrade, later to become King of Norway, considered it not only highly honorable but also a quite lucrative way of spending part of their youth as Varangians in Constantinople. Although initially the Scandinavians dominated the Varangian Guard, they became progressively outnumbered by the Saxons following the occupation of England by the Normans in 1066 AD, and the Nemitzoi, as the Byzantines called the Bavarians.

Members of the Varangian Guard were known for their loyalty and the empire's citizens considered them to be more reliable bodyguards. They always remained mercenaries, however, whose loyalty depended on their remuneration. It was precisely for this reason that a Varangian Guard's salary was much higher than that of other soldiers. In essence, it could amount to 200 gold coins annually, and they were also entitled to a portion of the plunder from the expeditions. It is possible that they also had the right to engage in a kind of ritual pillage of the royal quarters following the death of an emperor. This guard's characteristic weapon was a heavy battleaxe. The unit's commander was the *Akolouthos*, who was also a Varangian, as were all the other officers under his command. Also, for practical reasons, Byzantine translators were attached to the unit, although many of the guardsmen had learned Greek.

The soldiers' salary and maintenance

From the 6th to the 9th Centuries, volunteers exclusively carried out the recruitment of conscripts. The offspring of old soldiers had the privilege of preferential acceptance. During the reign of Heraclius (610 AD – 641 AD) or, more probably, of Constance II (641 AD – 668 AD), military service was partly turned into an inherited obligation. This method of recruitment later developed into a fundamental source of labor for the "thematic" army. This army was divided into two categories of soldiers: the first one comprised trained warriors that were the nucleus of each "theme." The second category consisted of a number of militia units that were assembled when required to assist the regular units of the "thematic" army. The difference between the two categories remains vague, however. Obviously, the first one constituted the regular force of the "thematic" army, having soldiers that were trained for warfare, while the second one consisted of countryfolk, who were only recruited in the event of a national crisis. The "thematic" army troops were recorded on special lists, where their obligations *(strateia)* were also noted. Copies of these lists were kept in the "themes," in Constantinople, and in the *logothesion* ("ministry") responsible for military affairs. Even the regular army soldiers served, usually only on a seasonal basis, while the rest of the time they farmed their land. Some of them were permanently on duty, however, and, in this case, they lived on the money given by those who wished to be exempted from military service.

During the middle period (6th – 12th centuries), the soldiers of the Byzantine army were relatively well paid. With their salary and the land granted to them, as well as the tax exemptions and the possibility of extra profits from plunder, they were considered to be among the highest paid employees in the empire. The men of the "thematic" units received a salary *(roga)* of 12 to 18 gold coins annually, increased by one coin each year until attaining the highest sum after 12 years service. During a campaign, the soldiers were supported by the state with the *siteresia*, while they also kept part of any loot. The cavalry received forage for their animals *(chortasmata)*, while there were also extra rewards *(doreai)* they would receive, say, on the occasion of an anniversary or an exceptional event, such as the appointment of a new emperor. Soldiers that became invalids during their service received a pension, while a deceased soldier's widow was entitled to a gratuity, amounting, in the 9th century, to 360 gold coins.

Obviously, the officers received a higher salary. During the reign of Leon VI the Wise (886 AD – 912 AD), a *Dekarchos* was remunerated with 72 coins per year, the *Pentekontarches* with 144, and the *Komes* with 216. The generals' salaries were considerably higher, and were incremental in five stages of 360, 720, 1440, 2160 and 2880 golden coins per year. The *Tourmarchaes*, *Drungarioi* and *Centurions (Ekatontarchoi)* also appear to have been remunerated on a rising scale, depending on the salary of the general under whose command they served. These salaries were effective during the reign of Leon VI the Wise and then only in the Eastern provinces. Officers of the Balkan provinces were paid less and, probably, not from the imperial treasury but through the imposition of a tax in the provinces where they served. Apart from their wage, most of the "thematic" soldiers owned their own land, which also constituted their basic subsistence.

The practice of ceding land to the frontier troops had been in operation since the late 7th century. A portion of the cultivable plots in the frontier provinces was characterized as military land *(stratiotopia)* and was awarded to soldiers of the "thematic" army. According to a decree of Emperor Constantine VII *Porphyrogenitos* (913 AD – 959 AD), the land awarded to a member of the infantry should have a value of at least 144 gold coins and that of members of the cavalry 288 gold coins, although, in the late 10th century, the lowest value limit for the cavalryman's land was tripled. Soldiers of the "thematic" army had to live off their area of land and be available for military service. It was not necessary, however, that the owner of the land offer himself for military service, he could pay someone else to serve in his place, on condition that he also covered all expenses for equipment and subsistence. The military service corresponding to a plot of land could be shared between various owners who combined together in order to pay the expenses of the soldier's subsistence *(syndosis)*. Under no circumstances could they be exempted from the obligation of offering the owed service except when the land was sold or donated, in which case the military service obligation was transferred to the new owner. Yet because of the military service that related to a particular parcel of land, ownership also brought with it some associated tax exemptions.

Maintaining an army during a campaign was a particularly onerous obligation for the local inhabitants. From the 10th century, this burden actually increased, as "tagmatic" army units and mercenaries began to spend all winter in some provinces. The officials in charge of the collection of revenue, like all the empire's financial employees, were famed for their cruelty and avarice. During the 11th century, many powerful landowners and monasteries, by imperial decree, managed to become exempt from the obligation of maintaining the army, but these exemptions were not always recognized.

The practice of purchasing out of military service, either by the owners of military land or by other taxpayers, eventually prevailed as the state preferred to collect revenue rather than services rendered. This money was retained in Constantinople and could be used in times of need to pay foreign mercenaries or be spent for other purposes. This practice finally resulted in the neglect of the army and fostered the idea that, if necessary, the state was able to buy the services of foreign mercenaries. The use of mercenaries was progressively expanded to such an extent that the activity of the "themes" was first reduced to guarding fortresses and patrolling the borders, then the "thematic" army fell into neglect, and finally it ceased to exist altogether.

Emperor Basil II,
the Boulgaroktonos,
in military dress accepts
the subordination of the
Bulgars. His breastplate
(lorikion), consisting of
metal plates,
can be clearly seen.
(San Marco National
Library, Venice –
Biblioteca Nazionale
Marciana di Venezia)

The Byzantine army's armament
in the middle period

The Byzantine army's weaponry and other war matériel during the middle period were influenced by the wide variety of peoples surrounding the empire. From the 6th century, the Avars were the first to adopt the use of horse stirrups from the tribes of central Asia and this progressively spread to the imperial cavalry with some alterations to the breastplate and shape of the saddle. The breastplates of the middle period were called *klibania*, *zabai* or *lorikia* (from the Latin term *lorica*) and usually consisted of metal rings, plates, or scales. The most common type of breastplate was made from long rectangular or square plates, tied together with leather straps and fastened around the body. On some scale breastplates, the upper plates partially covered the ones beneath, however, the opposite, lamellar, was more common, that is, the lower plates covered the bottom of the upper ones. The breastplates made of plates usually covered the person's torso. In rare instances, breastplates had sleeves made of the same material, or even an apron reaching to the knees. In other cases, the shoulder armor was made of special metal pieces, the *flamouliskia*, decorated with small, colored ribbons to make them more impressive. This type of breastplate offered better ventilation for the upper body along with more freedom of movement when compared to a cuirass beaten from a single sheet of metal, but they also provided a lower level of protection.

Up to the 7th century, troops serving in the heavy cavalry, in general, resembled the horsemen of Justinian's time. The overall tendency was to increase the heavy cavalry's armor. The main shock cavalry were the *klibanophoroi* and the *epilorikophoroi*, who wore heavy armor: a knee-length metal chainmail breastplate, often with sleeves reaching either to the elbow or the wrist. This type of breastplate was, probably, influenced by the armored heavy cavalrymen from the East. Over this breastplate, the horsemen wore a thick tunic (*epilorikion*) designed to cushion the force of enemy blows. In some instances, they also wore a similar tunic (*kabadion* or *bambakion*) under the breastplate, although this was more common in the infantry than the cavalry. A metal helmet, called *korys* or *kassis*, and a small shield held on the left side, supplemented the cavalryman's armor. Until the 7th century a bow with arrows hung on the right side and a sword on the left would complement a trooper's weaponry with the main weapon being a long spear (light lance) carried in his right hand. From the end of the spear shaft hung a small pennant, the *flamoulon*. Compared to previous centuries, horse armor had also been reinforced – they were protected on the breast, flanks and neck. It is also possible that the horses in the front rank of the battle line wore heavier armor than those in the rear ranks. However, only a very small portion of the army wore this type of heavy armor. The remainder of the cavalry simply wore tunics made from metal plates or leather. From the 7th century, cavalrymen became more specialized as either lancers or archers, fighting in mixed units deep enough to allow archers to shoot in support of front rank lancers.

The heavy infantry also wore heavy armor, consisting of a breastplate, helmet, greaves and a large shield, either circular or oval and up to 1.5 meters wide, to ensure better protection. Their offensive weapons were predominantly spears and swords. Beneath the breastplate they usually wore a hardened cloth tunic (*kabadion* or *bambakion*) to cushion the force of any blows. It is possible that the shields of the first line infantrymen were also equipped with a central boss. To protect their hands, the soldiers wore *cheiropsella*, *cheiromanika* or *manikelia*. On the legs they wore a type of greave called *podopsella* or *chalkotouba*, which afforded

The Byzantine army attacking a Syrian city. (Illuminated manuscript from John Skylitzes' chronicle, National Library, Madrid)

protection from ankle to knee. The armor for the hands and legs were made from either metal (iron or copper) or wood. Rear ranks were probably less well armored than this. The light infantry wore hardened cloth tunics instead of a breastplate and were armed with a smaller shield and light spears or a bow instead of a heavy spear. Their mission was to skirmish in front of the heavy infantry and then retire behind, supporting them with missiles. Thus, it was more important for their armor to be lighter and more flexible.

During the successive centuries of Arab expansion (from the 7th to the 10th centuries), a soldier's equipment became his own responsibility, at least for those serving in the forces of the "thematic" army. To enable them to buy their weapons, the soldiers received a special payment, but they often augmented this with their own money, especially if they wished to buy a better quality item. Some of the armor emanated from the state factories, as in earlier Roman times, which ensured some uniformity in the soldiers' appearance. In some cases, however, especially in the provinces, orders for the manufacture of war matériel were specifically awarded to local factories, resulting in regional differences. Eventually, the operation of the state factories declined and various local factories took over the manufacture of arms, especially for the "thematic" army. During the 7th century, all the state arms industries were occupied by the Arabs or were closed down, apart from those in Constantinople. There could still be found some factories in Asia Minor, but this is rather doubtful. The person in charge of the capital's blacksmith workshops was the Chief Armorer, but it is unknown if he had any involvement in the production of equipment for the "thematic" army. His factories mostly produced arms for the "tagmata" serving mainly in Constantinople. The supply of warhorses and pack animals was ensured through the collection of animals as a type of tax, by purchase at fixed prices and/or through the state stud farms *(metata)*. The latter were initially situated mainly in western Asia Minor. During the 12th century, however, due to the empire's loss of important territory in the region, most of them were transferred to the Balkan provinces and were renamed *chartoularata*, as the person in charge for them was the *Megas* (Grand) *Chartoularios* (in earlier times he was called "Chartoularios of the Stable").

By the 10th century, few changes in the armor of the imperial soldiers had taken place although new heavy shock units were instituted. The cavalry's double-edged sword was replaced with a single-edged weapon of the same length as the old *spathion* (longsword) that had been used until then. The round shields became much larger and eventually acquired a tear-drop shape reminiscent of the Norman almond-shaped shields. In the "thematic" army, some of the metal armor was replaced with hardened cloth, a turn of events that underlines the gradual neglect of these units to the advantage of the "tagmatic" army forces. The cavalry of the "thematic" army already used different types of breastplate, dependent on the financial viability of each horseman. They predominantly wore the *klibanion*, which reached to the waist, although some horsemen had the longer, metal *lorikia*. The *klibania* were usually made of iron, consisting of petal-shaped or small flake-shaped plates that were fixed to skin or cloth to produce a compact armor. The horsemen that wore *klibania* were called *klibanophoroi*. Some horsemen also wore a loose cloak *(epilorikion)* over the breastplate and were called *epilorikophoroi*. The *epilorikion*, made of hardened cloth, was sleeveless and protected the horseman's body, especially in light cavalry units, where the breastplates were virtually non-existent or of poor quality. Moreover, the *epilorikion* also protected the horsemen's armor from rain and humidity. The reconnaissance units used them as a kind of camouflaged combat clothing, as they wore dark colored *epilorikia* to prevent the enemy from spotting them easily. Some soldiers wore an *epanoklibanon*, a tunic adapted to the breastplate that, while not offering much protection, did help in the recognition of various units because of the different colors. In lightly armed units, the metal helmets were substituted with another type of head covering made of skin or hardened cloth. These horsemen also carried a bow along with arrows and a light shield.

Similar changes also occurred in the infantry's armor. It is possible that the soldiers who could afford better armor preferred to buy a horse so that they would be included in cavalry units; consequently the armor of those remaining in the infantry was relatively meager. Moreover, in the middle period (6th – 12th centuries) more emphasis was placed on the use of cavalry while the infantry was used mainly for guarding camps, cities and fortresses or for taking part in ambushes. Gradually, the "thematic" infantry lost its prestige and many military commanders considered them unreliable, believing that its soldiers were undisciplined and only fought with the thought of loot as their underlying motive. This mentality resulted in the neglect of both the organization and equipment of the infantrymen who, in consequence, wore only minimal, essential armor and even that was of sub-standard quality. The disadvantage of heavy armor was not only the cost, but also the need for constant maintenance i.e. keeping it safe and dry to prevent rust forming, a fact that limited its use to just the elite forces. The majority of the troops wore felt breastplates (thick cloth made from compressed animal hair) or ones made of textile *kentoukla (pilota kentoukleina)*. Many infantry soldiers wore *kabadia* (over-garments) of cotton or *koukoulion* (inferior quality silk). These knee-length *kabadia* were very thick and had short sleeves. In most cases, the metal helmets were replaced with cheap ones made of hardened cloth. These head coverings, made of felt or skin, were called *kamelafkia* and they usually had an additional leather cover to protect the neck. The heavy infantry shields were round or, in some cases, triangular or square, whereas the light infantry carried smaller round shields. The imperial infantry troops were armed with spears, swords, battleaxes and *kontaria*, spears that were longer than those of the previous period. The longer spears ensured that the infantry could use them to form an impenetrable barrier capable of resisting an attack by enemy cavalry.

Illustration of the campaign of the sovereign of Kiev against Constantinople in the middle of the 10th century. (Illuminated manuscript from John Skylitzes' chronicle, National Library, Madrid)

A battle between the Byzantines and the Arabs in Sicily during the 10th century. (Illuminated manuscript from John Skylitzes' chronicle, National Library, Madrid)

In contrast, the armor of the elite forces that constituted the imperial *tagmata* or extrs heavy cavalry of the *kataphraktoi* was quite different, and had been particularly favored by Nikephoros Phocas (963 AD – 969 AD). The *tagmata* were regularly supplied by the central government and it is possible that they were always given preference over the "thematic" army forces in both the soldiers' and horses' equipment. The most heavily armored cavalry force was the *kataphraktoi* that received its name from their heavy armor. The *kataphraktoi* of the 10th century wore a metal *klibanion* (breastplate), made of interlocking rings or plates. The hands were protected by reinforced silk gloves covered by metal plates. From waist to knees they were protected by hardened, padded cloth reinforced with metal, while the lower part of the legs were protected with copper greaves. Above the *klibanion* they wore an *epilorikion*. On the head they wore a steel helmet, with a chain mail curtain protecting the sides of the head. The horse barding was made of hardened padded cloth or skin and metal plates that covered almost the entire animal, protecting its neck, chest, and flanks. In specific cases, the hoofs were also protected from injury by special metal plates. The advantage of both the soldiers' and the horses' armor was that it did not have to be worn as a complete outfit. Some parts could be left in the camp if a mission did not require their use. The offensive weapons of the *kataphraktoi* included *apelatikia* or *vardoukia* ("maces") reinforced with three, four, or six flanges, a *paramerion* ("single-edged sword") and a *spathion* ("longsword"). The *apelatikion* was the basic weapon of the Byzantine heavy cavalry and infantry, who handled it to incredible effect, so much so that, according to contemporary sources, there were cases when hostile troops took flight as soon as they saw the *kataphraktoi* brandish their *apelatikia*.

The empire's neighbors to a large extent influenced the organization of the Byzantine *kataphraktoi*. Some elements of their armor were almost identical to the equipment of the Turkish and Magyar horsemen. The kataphraktoi fought in mixed units together with heavily armored horse archers and were mainly used for rupturing enemy lines. They did not attack at the gallop as Western knights and were very expensive to maintain. They numbered only two units of less than 400 men each. By the 11th century, they had ceased to exist due to their high cost. From then on, the only true shock cavalry available to Byzantium came from western-style knights, originating from the Komnenian dynasty which was supported by mercenary western knights. Indeed, units of the Byzantine select *tagmata*, the *Athanatoi* ("Immortals"), were trained in the techniques of the knights' battle tactics. The Court of Emperor Manuel I (1143 AD – 1180 AD) particularly appreciated the western-style jousts, which was preferred by the emperor and his courtiers and replaced the traditional horse races in the Constantinople hippodrome. The result of this was that, by the 11th century, the Byzantine heavy cavalry resembled the knight armies of western Europe a great deal, while the light cavalry and infantry were armed like their counterparts in the eastern empire, with breastplates of skin or hardened cloth reinforced with metal plates or rings at the most susceptible points, along with head coverings of the same materials.

The organization of the campaigns and the marches

During the middle period (from the 7th - 12th centuries) Byzantine army tactics provided for three types of campaign. The first was to relocate the army from the capital to a region that had been invaded by hostile forces and was seriously threatened. The second was to mount offensive operations on foreign territories with the usual goal of occupying a place of military importance. The emperor himself often participated on these operations, as the commander of the elite *tagmata* regiments that were usually stationed in the capital. The third type was mounting small-scale offensive or defensive operations along the borders in order to repulse intruders or raid hostile territories for plunder, whether in retribution for earlier raids or just to harass them. A campaign was carefully prepared long before it began. During the preceding months, the army's route was carefully laid down and those areas through which it would pass were clearly defined. The "thematic" forces were called upon to participate in the campaign and to rendezvous with the imperial army's main expeditionary corps. At predetermined points, large supply depots were established with this being the responsibility of the *Protonotarioi* of the corresponding "themes." These depots were usually fortified cities or other safe areas, which were also convenient for the inspection of the army as there would be level ground that was suitable for parades and military exercises. The "thematic" unit soldiers had to maintain themselves with their own supplies during their relocation to these bases. Only after their arrival at these predetermined concentration points and the integration of their unit with the rest of the army were they issued with supplies from the army depots that had been assembled to support the campaign.

When the Byzantine army was in hostile territory, it constructed fortified camps to ensure its security. The campsite was chosen by the campaign's commanding officer, after he had been informed about the terrain by the reconnaissance scouts ranging far ahead of the army. Basic conditions for setting up camp were the existence of sufficient water and adequate forage for the horses, as well as the possibility of the site being easily defended. Specialist officers, the *Mensouratores*, had the responsibility of setting up these camps. It was very likely that a "mensourator" accompanied each *bandon*, or any other similar sized units, and their work was supervised and coordinated by a senior officer. The camps were protected by moats and stockades, the latter constructed from trees that had been cut close by, or even from the infantry's spears and shields. Archers guarded the camp's gates, while patrols and sentinels maintained checks around the perimeter and also in the interior. Entrance to the camp and movement between different points required the use of passwords, usually the names of Saints or other words connected with the Orthodox Christian tradition. Each unit camped in a predetermined place, usually around its commanding officer's tent. The infantry units set up their camp around the outer walls with the cavalry and their horses beside them. In the center of the camp were the lodgings of the campaign's commander-in-chief and his staff. Surrounding these tents, the general's or, if present, the emperor's guard set up their tents. In special cases, two defensive precincts were built, especially if the emperor was present. Around his lodgings would be the tents of the imperial *tagmata*, while the responsibility for his safekeeping was maintained by the *Drungarios* of the Guard, some of the highest dignitaries of the emperor's bodyguard.

On the march, as with the setting up of the camps, the army advanced in well-organized units, usually with the expeditionary corps in front, followed by the supply train, the flanking forces, the vanguard and, finally, the rearguard. Just before the center of the main part of the army walked the general in charge of the campaign with his elite soldiers *(spatharioi)* followed by their personal baggage. If the emperor participated in a campaign, he would be mounted and accompanied by his courtiers. In this case, elite cavalry forces would be responsible for his protection. Each *droungos* or *tourma* was under the command of the corresponding commanding officer, followed by his bodyguard and the units' standards. Some distance in front of the whole force were the scouts, accompanied by local guides. The configuration of the army's formation changed depending on the terrain, be it level, mountainous, or if there were narrow, dangerous defiles, from which direct hostile attacks could be launched. Specialist officers, called *Doucatores*, had the duty of planning the details of the march. They were usually selected because of their knowledge of the territories through which the army marched. Particular emphasis was placed on reconnaissance and gaining in-depth knowledge of the terrain. Before the army advanced across any given area of country, units of light cavalry, which included the *Doucatores* and the *Mensouratores*, had already checked the way forward. During the advance of the bulk of the expeditionary corps, units of lightly armed cavalry and infantry protected its flanks. If the army was required to pass through a narrow passage, where the troops could only proceed on a frontage of just one or two files, the horsemen dismounted and proceeded on foot in the center of the formation. In these cases, the scouts would have thoroughly checked the area very carefully and, if the army intended to return by the same route, a small force was left behind to guard it. The overwhelming defeat at Myriokefalon in 1176 AD was due, to a large extent, to the failure to detect a narrow passage where the Seljuks lay in ambush. In some instances when narrow passages had to be negotiated, prisoners of war were often used as human shields.

Each unit was followed by the troops' pack animals, which carried their tents and other personal belongings, the transport of which was the responsibility of the soldiers themselves. Small groups of soldiers would usually pool their money in order to purchase one or more animals and to pay the animals' attendant. Few soldiers though could afford to possess their own animal and servant. This primarily applied to the "thematic" army units, while the transportation of the personal belongings of those serving in the *tagmata* regiments was usually on the backs of the army's pack animals. The convoy, called *touldon* or *touldos* which carried the entire army's supplies (siege engines, provisions, and weapons) was usually positioned at the tail of the procession when crossing empire territory. However, when the Byzantine army was in hostile territory, the *touldon* was positioned in the center of the procession and a special force was assigned to guard it. The *touldon* was, understandably, the slowest part of the column as it included, apart from the pack animals (donkeys and mules), carts drawn by oxen. A common principle when moving the expeditionary corps, from organized invasion armies to small units intended for plunder and harassment, was to leave behind large convoys and their escorts while crossing hostile territory. The majority of the supplies were usually left at the last important depot on empire territory, with the *Protonotarios* of the corresponding area being responsible for its safekeeping. Provisions and ammunition, such as arrows, weapons, and siege engines, were given priority for transportation over any other supplies. In some cases, even the personal tents of the junior officers could be left behind. A quantity of supplies could decisively impede the speed of the army during a march. In 1176 AD, during its march to Myriokefalon, the Byzantine army was accompanied by 3,000 carts, which included siege engines for the attack on Ikonion (modern day Konya) and the emperor's baggage. This huge column seriously impeded the movement of the army in the region's mountainous passages.

The distance covered by a military force depended on its composition (cavalry or infantry), the territory being crossed, as well as the conditions in which it operated. Large armies were cumbersome and could usually cover a distance of just 12 - 30 kilometers per day although, usually, it was around 20 kilometers per day. The more flexible cavalry forces could cover up to 75 kilometers per day. Naturally, infantry units were much slower, usually covering around 4.5 kilometers per hour, even less if over mountainous terrain. In some instances, the army column could extend over many kilometers, depending on the size of the force and the terrain being crossed. A force of 5,000 infantrymen, with a five-man frontage during a march, extended for two kilometers. The same applied

Siege of a Syrian city by Nikephoros Phocas. (Illuminated manuscript from John Scylitzes' chronicle, National Library, Madrid)

*SCUTATOS (**SHIELD-BEARER**) HEAVILY ARMORED FRONT-RANK
INFANTRY (950 AD – 1000 AD)*
*The defensive armor of the heavily armed infantrymen, seconded to the
military units stationed in Constantinople, included a Turanic one-
piece construction helmet over a mail coif, a full-length mail
lorikion, scaled cuirass, segmented arm guards, lamellar
shoulder protections and a convex oval body shield (scutari).
His primary offensive weapon was the spear (kontarion) fitted
with a long blade and a cornel or oak shaft, suitable
for penetrating light armor (or the bodies of horses
behind a solid shield wall). (uniform research
and reconstruction by Christos Giannopoulos)*

for a force of 1,000 cavalrymen, which advanced in two files. So, an army of 10,000 infantrymen and 5,000 horsemen extended for at least 14 kilometers, probably even more if one takes into consideration the small gaps between the units and the space allowed for the *touldon* and other units that were either ranged forward as scouts or along the flanks. It was very difficult to synchronize the pace of a force consisting of a combination of people and animals and a lot of effort was required from the troops and officers, as well as the pack animal attendants. The care of the horses was also another special factor impeding the pace of the march. Horses required regular breaks for rest and food, and one day per week to recover, as an extended, continuous march wore down their hoofs and backs and could render them temporarily or permanently unusable. In an emergency, though, the army could force the pace. In 995 AD, Basil II the Boulgaroktonos (976 AD – 1025 AD) led an army of 40,000 men from Constantinople to Aleppo (Halab in northern Syria) in just 20 days. This route usually required 60 days at the regular pace. The drawback was that, by the end of the march, only 17,000 of the Byzantine force managed to reach Aleppo, the rest left trailing behind as stragglers. (The above mentioned facts about Byzantine army marches can be found in *Warfare, State and Society in the Byzantine World, 565 – 1204* by John Haldon, London, 1999, pp. 158 – 166.

The army's conduct in battle

The Byzantine generals usually preferred to avoid offering open battle, unless they were absolutely certain of victory. Before each battle, the general would have ensured that he had secured a way of retreat for his troops and that his camp was sited properly, being in no danger of capture by the enemy. During preparations for the ensuing conflict, the Byzantine scouts would have maintained a continuous watch on the enemy, while reconnoitering suitable sites to lay ambushes. When an army left camp for the forthcoming battle, the pathfinders were sent ahead, followed by lightly armed skirmishers. The pathfinders would carefully check the field for traps or ambushes. The cavalry forces were accompanied by a number of horses without riders, in case some horsemen needed to replace their mounts during the course of the battle. These horses, however, were mainly intended for officers and couriers. The largest number of the spare animals remained safe in camp. In addition, a certain number of pack animals, loaded with weapons, mainly arrows and spears, followed the army. Usually, each unit's movements during the battle were carefully thought out beforehand with each commanding officer being informed of the required positioning of his soldiers.

Before the start of battle, the army's priests blessed the standards and celebrated Mass, praying for victory. While forming up the forces, the classic divisions of center, left center, and right center was applied. Once all the forces were in their designated battle positions, lightly armed, mobile, units were positioned on the flanks for protection against any attempt by the enemy to surround them. The reserves were positioned behind the main army formation, while the general retained a small reserve force in close proximity, to be used as an emergency, quick reaction force, during the battle. During the 10th century, light cavalry forces were positioned in front of the main bulk of the army, to shield it from the enemy. The most pivotal positions in the formation were usually given to units of the "tagmatic" army, as the "thematic" army troops were considered less disciplined and unreliable. In some cases during the 10th century, the "thematic" infantry units actually remained at the rear, acting as a protective square around the supplies. This square formation could also be used as a cavalry refuge in the event of the battle developing badly.

Once the lines of the battle array had been formed, the army stood in complete silence. The Byzantines believed that when an army was lined up in silence and, most of all, in an orderly manner, it would strike its opponents with awe, especially the barbarians who, when making war, did so as disorganized, screaming hordes. This complete silence reigned until the start of the battle, when the soldiers shouted a battle cry. There were various cries for any circumstance, usually accompanied by an invocation for help from God. As stated earlier, the empire considered itself to be a God-protected state and its citizens believed that God, the Virgin Mary, and the military Saints protected and assisted its army. During the 10th century, the soldiers would cry "Lord Jesus Christ have mercy on us." When the Byzantine forces consisted of mercenaries, they were also allowed to shout their own battle cries, even if they were not Christians, as often was the case with the Turks. During the battle, special emphasis was also placed on the use of drums and trumpets, especially when facing the barbarians, as these were impressed and terrified by the sound of drumming. Indeed, in some cases, enemies, influenced by the intensity of sound, believed that they were facing more troops than in reality. Maintaining discipline following an enemy's retreat was considered very important because if discipline broke down, the troops could be lured into a headlong pursuit and fall into an ambush. These rules were applied for the Byzantine army's battles throughout most of the 11th century. Then, because of the increased use of foreign mercenaries, other tactics were also adopted, depending on the method of fighting to which they were accustomed.

Sieges and raids

The organized campaigns were usually directed at a city or fortress with the aim of evicting an enemy from that particular territory. Moreover, in the disputed border territories, the possession of a fortress was important for the control of the nearby region. In these cases, the army arrived prepared for siege with all the necessary machinery and other matériel being transported by supply train *(touldon)*. During the sieges, tactics similar to those of the first period (4th - 7th centuries) were applied. When the army reached the fortress that was its objective, the officers first set about securing its protection by having the troops construct a well-fortified camp. Following this, the fortress was blockaded on each side, to prevent any re-supply of provisions and reinforcements. If there was sufficient time, the besiegers would wait until the food of the besieged ran out, so forcing them to surrender. If time was of essence, however, they were forced to employ other methods to overcome the defenses of a city or fortress quickly, such as siege engines, in order to break down part of the walls, or by assault. Even if the Byzantine army possessed highly sophisticated siege engines, they were rarely used. The military leaders preferred to avoid a long siege by forcing, or luring the enemy out of the city to face the besiegers in open battle or creating terror and/or dissension among the besieged citizens, thus obliging them to surrender. If all these methods failed, the besiegers would attempt a direct assault on the walls of

*Another scene
showing a siege
of a medieval town.
(Miniature painting
from John Skylitzes'
chronicle, National
Library, Madrid)*

the fortress. Before the attack, the army engineers attempted to undermine the walls by digging underground galleries beneath them. At the appropriate time, they then set fire to the wood used in the construction of the galleries, thus causing the collapse of the corresponding section of the walls. The most important siege undertaken by the Byzantine army of the middle period (6th to 12th centuries) was that of Chandaka, the Saracen pirates' base on Crete. The city was besieged and occupied by Nikephoros Phocas in 949 AD.

When the Byzantines conducted small-scale raids across the empire's eastern borders or confronted similar incursions by the Arabs or Turks, a different type of organization was required than that used in large-scale campaigns. In general, the "thematic" forces, whose duty it was to protect the borders, tended to move fast and take advantage of any opportunity to attack the enemy, without wasting time waiting for reinforcements. Hostile raids were divided into three primary categories. The first category of raids concerned surprise attacks by small groups of cavalrymen. In this case, the basic mission of the forces protecting the borders was to locate the invaders as soon as possible and drive them back or even trap them. The aim was to eliminate the intruders or force them to return to their base without plunder.

The second category of raids concerned large-scale raids that usually took place in August or September. The intruders' forces usually came from the frontier Arabic regions of Syria and Cilicia and consisted of regular army and fanatic Muslims, who wanted to annihilate the infidels. In this case, the army protecting the borders had to estimate quickly how large the hostile forces were, what route they intended to follow and when they would move. In the event that a Byzantine military governor could determine the route of the hostile raid, he made sure of the evacuation of the regions through which the invaders would pass. If the invasion had already begun, however, the imperial army continuously observed the enemy, following the enemy's main force and

eliminating any smaller groups diverging from it. The soldiers ambushed the enemy at any suitable site while, at the same time, *Akrites* occupied all the water wells. The objective was to annihilate the enemy forces in their camps and to wipe out any small units that had diverged from them to gather supplies or plunder. Particular emphasis was laid on the preparation of ambushes by which imperial forces could intercept the enemy raid or surprise them after a raid, when the enemy was moving slowly due to the amount of plunder they carried. In such an event, the Byzantines were able to recover a large portion of the acquired loot and thus deter the enemy from continuing the operation. Open battle was only offered if the imperial forces' dominance was guaranteed.

The third type of raid was the surprise invasion, which usually took place before the threatened regions could be evacuated. In this case, the "thematic" army would pretend that it planned to lure the opponent into open battle. By doing this, the invaders were forced to keep their main force assembled rather than divide it up to pillage an extended area. Thus, the imperial forces were allowed a little time in order to evacuate any threatened regions.

The empire, however, was not confined to the defense of the frontier regions. Along the eastern borders, the *Akrites* forces attempted to harass the Arabs by mounting raids into their territory. To conduct these raids, the local governors organized small groups of elite soldiers, called *trapezitai* or *trasinarioi*. A similar role was played by the *chonsarioi* along the empire's Balkan borders even if these do not appear to have been members of the regular "thematic" army but mercenaries, who could move more independently than the central military administration. The military governors of the Balkan "themes," moreover, did not particularly trust the *chonsarioi* and avoided revealing their plans to them, while specialist officers undertook the task of watching over their movements.

The aim of the Byzantine raids was usually the destruction of fortified enemy stations or even an important center, and plundering their territories. Particular

Illustration of a battle between Byzantines and Bulgars. (Illuminated manuscript from Constantine Manasses' chronicle, Apostolical Library, Vatican)

emphasis was also laid on continually operating a network of observers and spies. Scouts with a very good knowledge of the terrain and the enemy's tactics constantly checked those points where the army would be expected to pass and those regions where hostile forces could unexpectedly appear. Merchants and any person(s) who crossed a region without raising suspicion could be used as spies for collecting valuable data about the position of the enemy and their possible intentions. Prisoners of war were also an important source of information and, often, small-scale raids were carried out with the aim of capturing some citizens from enemy territory for interrogation. Soldiers from the "thematic" forces were recruited for these raids, while some officers undertook the periodic duty of checking the activities of the scouts.

The extensive use of mercenaries during the reign of the Komnenian dynasty

The progressive weakening of the "thematic" military forces, which finally led to their complete disbandment, accelerated during the 11th century. This phenomenon owed much to the severe tax policies of the period from 1030 AD to 1060 AD and to the perception that, after the recapture of many provinces and the creation of ostensibly constant borders in Asia Minor and along the Danube, the Byzantine state no longer required its old frontier forces. The empire primarily depended on the forces of the tagmatic regiments stationed in the capital and other major fortified cities while, during campaigns, more mercenaries were recruited. These mercenaries, paid by the empire, came from many nations both East and West, including Georgians, Alans, Cumans, Pechenegs, Serbs, Turks, and Magyars but with particular emphasis on recruitment from the East. Another special characteristic of the 11th century was the increasing use of mercenary knights from Western Europe, mainly Franks, Normans, and other Germanics. Mercenaries also dominated the emperor's bodyguard, the largest number of which constituted the elite corps of Varangians. Initially, the Varangians came from the Scandinavian countries but, from the middle of the 11th century, the majority of them were Anglo-Saxons. A very similar practice of using mercenaries also prevailed for naval operations, for which they primarily used Venetian ships that, in return, were granted commercial privileges in the empire's territories.

An illuminated manuscript showing several types of siege engine demolishing a fortified wall. (Vatican Library)

The result of this practice was the near total dependence of the empire on foreign mercenaries. During the second half of the 11th century, the Byzantine state was not in position to carry out large-scale offensive or defensive operations without the contribution of mercenary forces. During the period of the Komnenos dynasty, foreign mercenaries played a very significant role in every important operation by the Byzantine army. When Emperor Manuel I Komnenos (1143 AD – 1180 AD) besieged the Normans at Brindision (modern Brindisium in Italy) in

The Emperor Basil I, shown mounted, inspecting his troops. (Illuminated manuscript from John Skylitzes' chronicle, National Library, Madrid)

1156 AD, his army consisted mainly of Norman and Italian mercenaries and a combination of Alans, Cumans, and Georgians. In 1145 AD, the same emperor had an agreement with Emperor Conrad of Germany for Conrad to supply 500 knights. A similar agreement was also reached with the leader of the Serbs, who agreed to offer 500 soldiers for the empire's campaigns in Asia Minor and 2,000 for the campaigns in Europe.

The disbanding of the frontier forces altered the situation in Asia Minor during the second half of the 11th and the whole of the 12th centuries, when continuous military activity occurred in the region, as had also happened along the eastern borders with the Arabs from the 7th until the 10th centuries. The empire's borders, however, were no longer along the eastern part of Anatolia but along the western part of its central region. The coasts of northern Asia Minor and the plains of its eastern regions fell easy prey to the new enemy, the Seljuk Turks, who had settled in the center of Anatolia and made frequent forays into the empire's territories. In order to confront this threat, the empire instituted a more static defense. Strong fortresses were built at a number of sites of strategic importance and the fortifications of the most important cities were also strengthened. Those fortifications could force the approach of the invaders to the coasts and be used as bases for conducting counter-attacks.

Henceforth, hostile raids were faced with desultory resistance and not so much by local forces but rather by the "tagmatic" army that moved from the large centers of Asia Minor or Constantinople itself. Some units remained in the frontier fortresses for extended periods as guards, assigned to intercept any intruders. Often, however, they lacked the basic mobility to accomplish their mission. The Seljuks, with small, flexible groups of horsemen, continuously conducted small-scale raids that, cumulatively, had a severe impact on the empire. The central administration in Constantinople, after contributing to the disbandment of the forces that, hitherto, had protected the borders, attempted to confront these raids with occasional forays by large, slow-moving "tagmatic" army forces, consisting mainly of mercenaries. It was an ineffective and shortsighted tactic, doomed to failure. The Angelos dynasty, that succeeded the Komnenos, hastened the weakening of the empire's military forces, thus facilitating its conquest by the Crusaders in 1204 AD.

The late Byzantine army (1204 AD – 1461 AD)

The last centuries of Byzantium

The Empire after the Fourth Crusade

The Fourth Crusade caused chaos throughout the Greek peninsula, breaking up the unity and relative stability that the Byzantine Empire had provided until then. The Crusaders' assault on Constantinople resulted in a large number of disruptive incidents in the Byzantine provinces, as many powerful local notables attempted to take advantage of the situation to create small hegemonies of their own. In addition, the Crusaders sought to create their own small states in Greece while the Bulgarians wanted to occupy the territories of Macedonia and Thrace. At the same time, in Asia Minor the Turks took the opportunity to expand into the last Byzantine territories.

St. Orestes' icon. His breastplate and a small part of the shield can be clearly seen. (Fresco-painting from Episkopi church at Eurytania)

The immediate aftermath of the Fourth Crusade was the creation of a number of Byzantine and Latin states around the Aegean Sea and in Asia Minor. Initially, the most important Latin state was the Empire of Constantinople, which included Thrace and the Asia Minor coast of the Bosporus. The Latin kingdom of Thessalonica was founded in Macedonia and Thessaly, while Attica with Boeotia and the Peloponnesus constituted independent hegemonies. The Byzantines tried to organize their reaction to the various hegemonies founded at that time. The most important of these was the Empire of Nicaea, which took its name from the Asia Minor city that was its capital. This state also included parts of northwestern Asia Minor. The Patriarch of Constantinople and Theodore I Laskaris (1204 AD – 1222 AD), who ascended the throne the same dramatic evening that the capital was captured by the Crusaders, had fled to Nicaea. Even if the Nicaean state was considered to be the only legitimate successor to the Byzantine Empire, the title was disputed by other Byzantine hegemonies. One of them was the Empire of Trebizond, created in 1204 AD by the descendants of the imperial Komnenos family on the northern coast of Asia Minor. Another Byzantine hegemony was the Despotate of Epirus, which initially showed exceptional dynamism and even managed to recapture Thessalonica from the Latins in December 1224 AD.

The Despotate of Epirus' successes were only temporary. The Nicaean Empire, however, managed to recapture Thessalonica during the reign of John III Vatatzes (1222 AD – 1254 AD)

BYZANTINE CAVALRYMEN DURING THE 13th-14th CENTURIES AD
This illustration was primarily based on information from "The Chronicle of Alexander the Great," a Byzantine manuscript from the 14th century AD. Particularly noticeable is the old-style scale armor of the mounted nobleman (probably a member of the imperial family) as well as that of his horse, the characteristic pectoral straps on the chests of both men, their wide-brimmed helmets (a typical Byzantine article of equipment during this period), and their large kite-shaped convex shields decorated with the two-headed eagle or Holy Cross pattern. (uniform research and reconstruction - illustration by Christos Giannopoulos)

who proved a very capable military leader and, in addition, managed to cause difficulties for the Latin empire of Constantinople, annexing large parts of its territories. Finally, however, the emperor who recaptured Constantinople was Michael VIII Palaiologos (1259 AD – 1282 AD), the founder of the last Byzantine dynasty. Michael VIII Palaiologos' reign was the final brilliant period of Byzantine history. Moreover, the first of the Palaiologos dynasty managed to recover the castles of Lakonia (in southeastern Peloponnesus), thus laying the foundations for the creation of the Despotate of Mystras in the Peloponnesus and the final recovery of the region by the Byzantines. The recovery of Constantinople, however, also had a number of negative consequences. The return of the capital to Constantinople removed the imperial government's interest from the Asia Minor provinces that were threatened by the Turks. The Palaiologos dynasty, furthermore, as members of the large landowners, had no wish to support the remaining small soldier/farmers, because these hindered the expansion of their properties. Thus, the last hope for the salvation of Byzantine Asia Minor was finally lost.

During Andronikos II Palaiologos' reign (1282 AD – 1328 AD), the Byzantines made a series of fatal errors. The emperor attempted to prevent Turkish expansion into Asia Minor by recruiting mercenaries from the West. He selected a group of Catalan mercenaries, the self-styled "Catalan Grand Company." Initially, the Catalans scored a number of successes against the Turks. Following this, however, they turned against the empire and ruthlessly ransacked Thrace and Macedonia. Finally, they turned their attention to Attica and Boeotia, conquering the Latin state there, causing extensive depredation across the empire's Balkan provinces. Despite this, Asia Minor still remained unprotected and, by the middle of the 14th century, most of it had been lost. Only some fortified cities remained under the control of the empire. Andronikos II's reign ended with a civil war between him and his grandson, Andronikos III Palaiologos (1328 AD – 1341 AD).

A general picture of Mystras. The town fortifications as well as the castle on top of the hill can be clearly seen.

In the middle of the 14th century, following Andronikos III's death, the Byzantine state was shaken by a second civil war, this time between the dead emperor's son, John V Palaiologos and John Kantakouzenos, a close associate of the deceased Andronikos III, who claimed the throne. Neither of the rivals hesitated to call on the Serbs and the Ottomans -a recently emerged Turkish tribe that occupied the northwestern part of Asia Minor- for assistance. Kantakouzenos finally managed to ascend the throne, albeit temporarily, as Emperor John VI from 1347 AD – 1354 AD, although at enormous cost. The Serbs took advantage of the situation to occupy a major part of Macedonia so the only possessions of the Byzantine state that remained were a part of Thrace and the Despotate of Mystras, in the Peloponnesus, along with a few Aegean islands.

The Expansion of the Ottomans

An even more disastrous development was the occupation by the Ottomans of the fortresses in Thrace. First, Tzymbi, on the Gallipoli Peninsula, was occupied in 1353 AD. The fall of Gallipoli itself followed a few years later. By 1362 AD, the Ottomans had expanded into the Evros Valley, occupying Didymoteichon, Adrianople, and Filippopoli (modern Plovdiv in Bulgaria). Thessalonica fell in 1387 AD and in 1389 AD, the Ottomans defeated the Serbs at the Battle of Kosovo. The invaders quickly expanded into the hinterland of the Balkans, while simultaneously applying a pincer movement around Constantinople. The Byzantine state attempted to react by seeking the dispatch of military assistance from the West. In order to ensure this help, the last of the Palaiologos dynasty was ready to accept the subjugation of the Orthodox to the Catholic Church. Two emperors, Manuel II Palaiologos (1391 AD – 1425 AD) and his son John VIII (1425 AD – 1448 AD) traveled to Western Europe in order to elicit help but, in the end, gained nothing more than promises.

In 1396 AD at Nikopolis in Bulgaria, the Ottomans defeated a powerful Crusading army that had been sent against them. At the same time, they began to exert more pressure on Constantinople, having as their ultimate goal to capture the Byzantine Empire's capital. The city was saved, temporarily, when, in 1402 AD, Tamerlane's Mongols defeated the Ottoman army at Ankara. The Byzantines tried to take advantage of the situation and, once again temporarily, recovered some lost territories, including Thessalonica. The Ottoman state, however, quickly recovered and recaptured all the regions it had lost. The only positive element to the first half of the 15th century was the demise of the Latin hegemony of the Peloponnesus. In 1430 AD, Constantine Palaiologos, who was later to be the last emperor of Byzantium, also managed to occupy the last fortresses in the hands of the Latins of the Peloponnesus (the remains of the Principality of Achaia created by the Franks in the 13th century). This small Latin state, however, over many years, had fallen into decay and was easy prey. The real force in the Balkans from then on was the Ottomans, whose expansionist policies could not be halted by any single Christian state.

St. Demetrius defends the walls of Thessalonica. The Saint's lorikion *can be clearly seen. The adherence to the military saints was connected to the Byzantines' total belief that God himself protected their state. (Reliquary of Vatopedi Monastery, Hagio Oros)*

In 1449 AD, Constantine Palaiologos ascended the throne, while, in 1451 AD, Mehmed II, who was determined to occupy Constantinople, ascended the Ottoman throne. Following two years of preparation, in 1453 AD, the Ottoman army appeared before the city walls. In Constantinople, Constantine Palaiologos had around 1,500 soldiers under his command. These troops were the remnants of the army of the Eastern Roman Empire. Another 3,000 Byzantines and about 3,000 Latins, mainly Venetians, Genoese, and Catalans, were added to them. Some of these were mercenaries, with the remainder fighting to protect their commercial interests. The Genoese mercenary, Giustiniani, who commanded a group of elite professional soldiers from Italy, held an important position in the organization of the defense of Constantinople. Against this meager force, Mehmed II commanded 150,000 troops and, for the first time during a large-scale siege, several heavy artillery pieces that caused significant damage to the ancient walls of Constantinople. It was obviously an unequal battle that finally culminated on the 29th May 1453 AD with the Turks occupying the city. The last emperor was killed in the fighting while commanding what was left of his army. The final sparks of the political existence of Byzantium were extinguished a few years later. In 1460 AD, Mystras was subjugated, followed by Trebizond on the 15th August 1461 AD. The more-than-a-thousand-year-old course of Byzantine Hellenism had expired. However, Byzantine moral fiber survived for some time with the Greeks who fled to the West in order to escape Turkish occupation. Among them were not only many scholars but also professional soldiers, who served in the western armies under the name *stradiotti*, a title emanating from the Byzantine term *stratiotes* ("soldier").

The organization of the Byzantine armies during the late period

Mercenaries in the late Byzantine army

During the late period, foreign mercenaries made up the largest part of the armies of the empire and of the Byzantine states that were created after the Fourth Crusade, although there were also indigenous troops serving in the armies of the various states. The foreign mercenaries came from different regions and nations of both east and west. Several contemporary historical sources report Italians, French, Germans, Catalans, English, Serbs, Bulgarians, Vlachs, Albanians, Georgians, Turks, Cumans, and Alans. The empire also used the *"gasmouloi,"* the offspring of the result of mixed marriages between the Latins and the Greeks, as mercenaries, especially in the navy. The majority of mercenaries did not permanently serve any particular Byzantine sovereign, but rather were engaged when their services were deemed necessary, mainly during the organization of a campaign or to deter a barbarian invasion. That said, there were also a number of mercenaries who carried out permanent guard duties in a city or fortress. In point of fact, during 1354 AD, Catalan mercenaries guarded a portion of the walls of Constantinople.

The extensive use of mercenaries during that period did not constitute a Byzantine peculiarity. On the contrary, it was particularly widespread, especially in

The ruins of the castle of Moglena (Almopia) in western Macedonia.

Western Europe, predominantly in neighboring Italy, where there was much civil unrest and inter city-state conflicts were quite frequent. In the West, powerful sovereigns either fought to defend their independence against treacherous neighbors or attempted to expand their power by force. These continuous conflicts were the root cause of the ever-increasing demand for mercenaries. Mercenaries, moreover, had the advantage that they were much better trained and were available at any moment, which, as a result, made them more effective in directly confronting a surprise attack. In contrast, the soldier-farmers required periods of rest in order to cultivate their lands or to deal with domestic affairs. They also required time to assemble and, even then, it was often that some would arrive insufficiently armed for action. Indeed, in some cases they failed to show-up at all, preferring to protect their properties and settlements. This, in fact, happened during the Mongol invasion of 1324 AD, when Emperor Andronikos III (1328 AD – 1341 AD) ordered the mobilization of the soldier-farmers, who, however, preferred to defend their own towns.

Many of the mercenaries (called *condottieri* in Italy) would assemble in large groups that, in the West, were called "free companies" and the Byzantines called *syntrophiai* (meaning "companies" – bands of men). These groups were usually composed of individuals of a common origin. Mercenaries operated under the strict statutes of the company to which they belonged, just as respectable craftsmen and professionals of that time all belonged to craft guilds and complied with the requirements of those organizations. Unlike those other craft guilds, however, each individual mercenary company operated under its own rules and usually offered its services under contractual arrangements between the group's leaders and its prospective employer. With the company rules as a base, the rewards were distributed depending on the rank and what each mercenary had offered. Mercenaries, like members of all the other professional guilds, had a particular sacred guardian; Saint George was venerated as the patron of the hired fighters. When a mercenary company had completed its "duty" in a certain place, it moved elsewhere in search of a new employer. Although mercenaries were much sought after in time of war, when peace prevailed their employers tried to get rid of them as soon as possible as they created disturbances with their violent behavior and rapacious attitude.

The extensive use of mercenaries caused significant damage to the Byzantine economy as the emperors were forced to drain the state funds in order to pay for their services. When state funds were insufficient, they resorted to using their personal wealth as well as church property and to imposing oppressive taxes. The *vigliatikon* constituted a type of tax for military purposes. In 1304 AD, Emperor Andronikos II (1282 AD – 1328 AD) imposed a new tax on the production of cereals, called *sitokrithon*, in order to ensure the payment of the mercenaries of the Catalan Grand Company. The income from the imposition of new taxes, however, was somewhat meager, as the emperors granted significant tax exemptions, mainly to monasteries and major landowners.

Paying the soldiers and the *pronoiars*

During the late period of Byzantine history, various methods of payment were developed for the soldiers, who were rewarded for their services with grants of land, money, or even some state revenues. In certain cases, soldiers were rewarded with a combination of all these. These grants were usually made on condition that, not only would the beneficiary continue to provide military services, but also those who succeeded them would do likewise. Soldiers also received extra gifts in the form of valuable objects. These gifts were usually awarded to those who had distinguished themselves in battle and were, usually, announced in advance. In 1350 AD, John VI Kantakouzenos (1347 AD – 1354 AD), at the siege of Vodena (modern Edessa in Greece), promised 288 golden coins to the first man to lower an enemy flag from the walls, and smaller sums to those who would closely follow him in the occupation of the city. Other gifts were also awarded to soldiers under particular circumstances, such as the nomination of a new emperor. In these cases, the offer of money, apart from the continuation of the old Roman tradition, also constituted a means of reassuring the loyalty of the mercenaries to the new emperor. In addition, an important part of a soldier's remuneration was loot. According to tradition, soldiers were eligible to a share of three fifths of the loot, while the emperor and the Grand Domesticos shared the remainder. In reality, however, the Byzantine armies of the late period were too ill-disciplined for restrictions to be imposed on them. They were not disposed to concede anything to their superiors, and very often they ended up quarrelling violently over the distribution of the loot.

Army catering took place via the depots that existed in castles and fortified cities. The local governors were in charge of gathering and distributing supplies. The local population was obliged to sell its produce to the state depots as well as to the army at prices lower than the market norm. This obligation was called *mitaton* and, in certain cases, was particularly onerous for the minor landowners and cultivators. The soldiers' weapons and horses were usually privately purchased although, in some instances, constituted a state commitment. It was also specified that the soldiers' weapons and horses had to be returned to the state if there were no heirs to succeed them in their military obligations.

The largest part of the empire's non-mercenary forces during the late period was composed of soldiers who by virtue of their military service, had been granted plots of land or other revenues. This system was called *pronoia* (meaning "providence") with the holders of the land called *pronoiars*. By this system, the state granted someone permission to collect certain state revenues, as a reward for the services offered.

The beneficiary of the *pronoia*, however, was not compelled to offer his military services for the entire duration of that institution. Usually, the pronoiars simply collected the income from the cultivation of the land that had been granted to them by the state. Villeins (farmers compelled to cultivate the land) did the actual farming and the pronoiars took a part of the crop for themselves and passed the required sum on to the state. Simlarly, the pronoiars could assign others to perform their military duties for them. Perhaps it was this arrangement that led to the distinction in Byzantine texts of that period between the term stratiotis, meaning "soldier" (the owner of the land who was obliged to offer his military service) and strateuomenos (the person who actually performed the required military service). Sometimes, the *pronoiars* came from the empire's transfer of a population to specified settlement sites. This happened in the case of the Cumans, as well as with groups of Tzakones who served in the light cavalry.

It is thought that the *pronoia* was not a hereditary institution, but was actually connected with the assignment of other services. Progressively, however, the holders of the land presented themselves as owners and began to neglect their obligations regarding owed services, while the state was unable to protect its interests. The central administration was not deprived of its responsibilities by this development as it converted a lot of *pronoiai* to hereditary, thus undermining the future of the Byzantine military organization. The start of the transformation of *pronoiai* into a hereditary institution took place during Michael VIII Palaiologos' reign (1259 AD – 1282 AD). By the middle of the 14th century, because of civil wars, the rival parties attempted to gain the support of the *pronoiars*, allowing them to bequeath the *pronoiai* to their heirs. At the same time, many *pronoiars* were exempted from the obligations they had undertaken. Thus, this institution declined and before the close of the 14th century, it had virtually collapsed, depriving the Byzantine state of its last soldiers/landholders. The remnants of the empire would, henceforth, have to depend on the services of mercenaries for its protection and defense.

The units and the administration of the army

The fighting prowess of the Byzantine forces during that period was remarkably low. Judging from various battles against the Latins, it can be seen that even small groups of determined knights could usually drive off much larger Byzantine armies. The army was divided into *allaghia*, large groups of soldiers, but without a strictly determined size. While the *allaghia* usually were numerically equivalent units, they did, however, consist of men of common

The ruins of Sidirokastron in Macedonia.

St. Nestor is depicted wearing a lorikion, *and sword, and carrying a shield. (painted fresco from St. Nicholaos Kasnitzes Church, Kastoria)*

origin. This is to say, there could exist only one *allaghio* covering all the mercenaries, or even separate *allaghia* for each group of mercenaries dependent on their national origin. The light, as well as the heavily armed or elite soldiers were assigned to separate *allaghia*. The terms *tagmata*, *lochoi*, *taxeis* or *syntaxeis* were also used, meaning specific parts of the battle line (left and right side, center) while not defining the type of units. The Byzantine armies at the beginning of the late period were relatively small, usually consisting of just a few thousand men. In 1211 AD, the Nicaean Empire had a battle array of 2,000 soldiers, 800 of which were western mercenaries. Progressively, though, the total numbers began to increase, especially from Michael VIII Palaiologos' reign (1259 AD – 1282 AD) onwards. This increase, though, mainly concerned the quantity rather than the quality of the troops.

The basis of the forces of the late Byzantine armies was the cavalry. The infantry forces were considered auxiliary and were scarcely mentioned in the headcount of the army's fighting men. At times, a military force consisted entirely of horsemen, especially when it was necessary to move fast. The horsemen were divided into light and heavily armed, who were still called *kataphraktoi*. The *kataphraktoi* were usually Byzantine *pronoiars* or members of the upper aristocracy; sometimes, Western European mercenary knights were used instead of heavily armed locals. The lightly armed horsemen were usually mounted archers from the East, mainly Turks, Alans, Cumans or *Tourkopouloi*, as the Christianized Turks were called. Most mercenaries were mounted but, in some cases, they were also accompanied by groups of infantrymen, primarily heavily armed soldiers or archers. The infantrymen were also divided into two categories, the light and the heavily armed. The heavily armed infantrymen were called *hoplites* and the rest *psiloi*. Those terms were taken from the classical texts of the great ancient Greek historians. The writers of the late Byzantine period probably used them in order to demonstrate their classical education and not because the corresponding types of soldiers were really called this. The *hoplites'* mission was usually the safekeeping of a fortress and took part in battles only when not enough horses were available. The lightly armed infantrymen were usually archers and mainly Byzantine in origin.

Better trained were the imperial guard forces, the nucleus of which continued to be, even in the late Byzantine period, the Varangian Guard. Its members, however, almost exclusively came from England, which the Byzantines of that period called "Celts." They continued to be armed with impressive battleaxes. Apart from insuring the safekeeping of the emperor, they had also undertaken the task of guarding the treasury and the palace prison, acting as the prisoners' warders and torturers. The indiscipline that dominated the Byzantine army, however, also influenced the emperor's bodyguard. A number of Varangians illegally demanded money from those wishing to enter

BYZANTINE CAVALRYMAN IN THE SERVICE OF THE PALAIOLOGIAN DYNASTY (LATE 14th CENTURY AD)

The last realistic representations of Byzantine military units come from "The Chronicle of Alexander the Great" (a Byzantine manuscript of the 14th century AD) as well as from relatively unknown hagiographies (paintings of holy images) from medieval churches in the Balkans. This particular cavalryman wears composite armor consisting of metal plates (klibanion) and chain mail according to the current Eurasiatic trend, which dominated the Balkan armies. He also wears a helmet with a broad brim, which protected him from sabre blows, and a full chain hood that covered the whole of his face save for his eyes. Metal disks protected his shoulders and arms, and he carries a triangular shield with a highly curved surface and leather band. The main offensive weapons depicted here are the Turkish scimitar, the straight double-edged western-type sword (only a small part of its scabbard can be seen in the illustration) and a *eusplachnia* (meaning "mercy" or "charity") type of dagger. (uniform research and reconstruction by Christos Giannopoulos)

the palace in order to submit a demand to the emperor's secretariat. The Varangian Guard existed until the beginning of the 15th century. After that time, no contemporary report exists concerning this elite unit. The reasons for its progressive dissolution were, on the one hand, the territorial shrinkage and the economic collapse of the empire that made service in Constantinople less attractive for the Anglo-Saxons and, on the other hand, perhaps it was the ongoing 100 Years War between England and France. This war began in the middle of the 15th century and it is likely that it prevented the transfer of mercenaries from England to Constantinople.

The emperors always took overall command of the empire's military forces. Some of them, such as John III Vatatzes (1222 AD – 1254 AD), Andronikos III and John VI Kantakouzenos (1347 AD – 1354 AD) led their army when on campaign. In contrast, other emperors, such as Michael VIII Palaiologos (1259 AD – 1282 AD) and his son Andronikos II (1282 AD – 1328 AD) preferred to assign the administration of the army to others. When the emperor took no part in the campaign, the army's administration was taken over by the *Megas* (Grand) *Domestikos*, who often was a close relative of the imperial family. The most important *Megaloi* (Grand) *Domestikoi* was John Palaiologos, brother of Michael VIII, Alexios Strategopoulos who recaptured Constantinople from the Latins in 1261 AD, and John VI Kantakouzenos, before ascending to the throne, a close friend of Andronikos III. In the Despotate of Mystras, the despot himself usually conducted the army's administration during military operations.

The senior officers of the late period were granted impressive, somewhat pompous titles that, however, did not correspond with their actual authority. The superior military ranks after that of the *Megas Domestikos* were those of the *Protostrator*, the *Megas Stratopedarches*, the *Megas Kontostaulos* and the *Megas Hetereiarches*. These titles were then awarded to various dignitaries, without regard to the actual service they carried out. In fact, the titles had more of a ceremonial use and simply underlined the emperor's appreciation for the title's holder. In some cases, a title was granted even without being accompanied by any actual duties. During the late period, all the senior officers were from powerful families of the Byzantine aristocracy and had strong bonds of allegiance to the imperial family. They conducted the army's general administration together with the emperor and the *Megas Domestikos*. Other dignitaries were the provincial governors, called *kefalai* ("heads"). The mercenary forces acted under the command of their own leaders, also mercenaries, who were usually of common origin with the soldiers they commanded.

The weapons and the campaigns

The Byzantine army's weapons during the late period were distinguished by their extensive variety. They were the result of numerous influences from both West and East, along with some indigenous remnants from the middle Byzantine period. The soldiers' armor mainly consisted of chain mail that covered their upper bodies. In some instances, they were fitted with sleeves but only to the elbow. The suit reached to just below the waist, although some reached just above the knees. These chain mail jerkins had no chain mail hood, the head being protected by a helmet. Chain hoods were often used independently from the chain mail jerkin. Over the chain mail jerkin, the wearer wore a piece of durable cloth, offering more protection. Sometimes, instead of the cloth, an additional breastplate, made of metal or hardened skin, was worn. The helmet was usually conical or onion-shaped and relatively tall. It had a level brim that could be wide or narrow and turned down. These helmets were manufactured from one or two pieces of metal. There were also conical helmets without brims. On the sides of helmet, the wearer could hang chain mail or even wear the helmet over the chain mail hood. However, simple round helmets, offering only basic protection to the wearer, were also used. Leather boots offered protection to the lower legs. The shields were usually wooden and triangular, curved from side to side. Their lower part was narrow in order to protect the knees of the horseman who carried it, while their upper part was wide in order to cover the arm and the left shoulder. When they were not using them, the soldiers would often hang their shields on their backs, sometimes upside down.

The above items mainly pertain to cavalrymen. The weapons of the infantry, a force considered of limited use or value at that time, were much simpler. Members of heavy infantry units were protected by knee-length tunics of durable cloth strengthened with metal parts, while members of the light infantry had no particular armor. They wore clothes identical to those of the farmers of the period, the class from which most of them came.

The basic offensive weapon of the late period was the sword, of which two main types were used. One was relatively thin and narrow at the tip, while the other one was a curved saber. Both the cavalry and the infantry used the lance. Also, the majority of troops of that time were competent in the use of bows. There were many soldiers capable of shooting arrows while riding a horse, especially in the Trebizond Empire. They owed this to the fact that they lived adjacent to and often fought against the Turkish mounted archers. The Byzantines were aware of the crossbow but seldom used it to its potential, although it came to be employed more often during sieges and in naval battles.

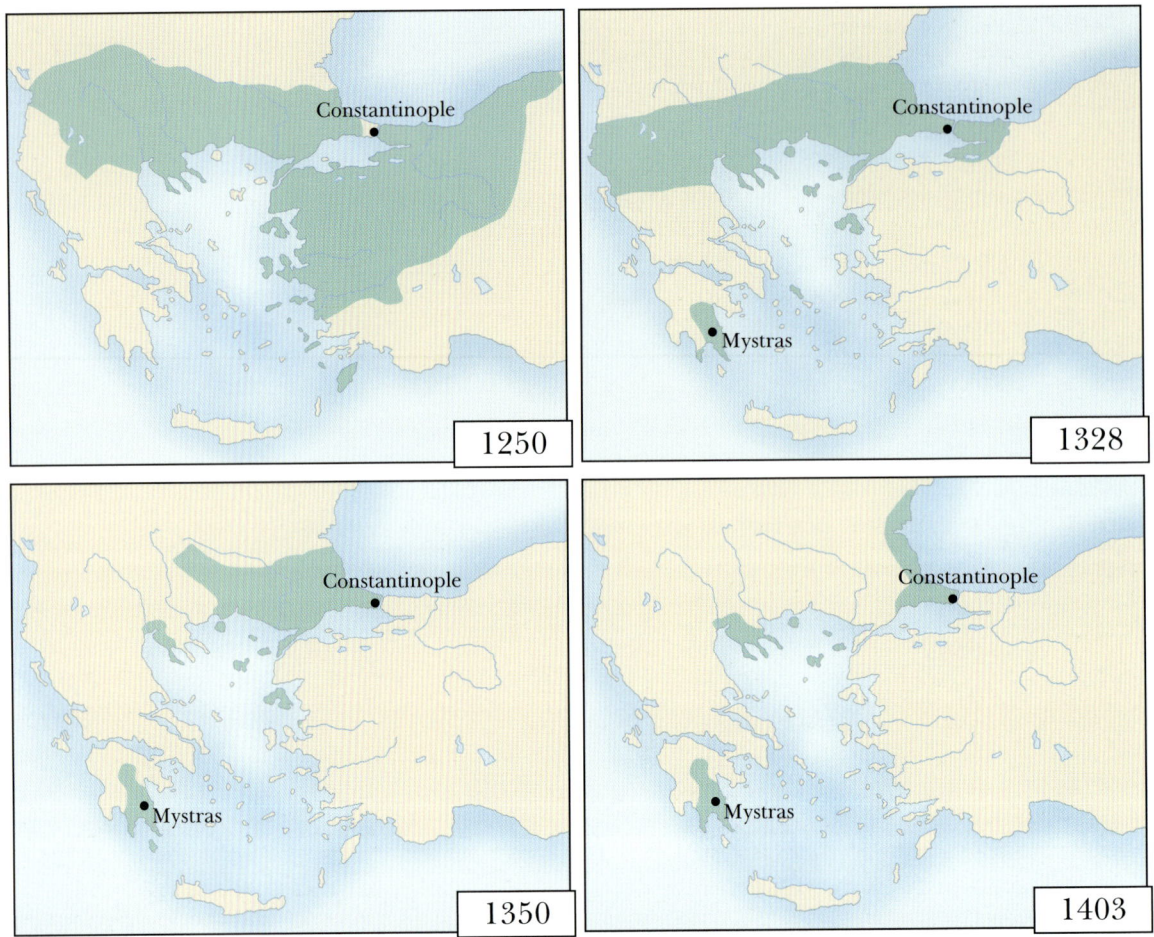

Byzantine territorial losses (1250 AD - 1403 AD).

During the late period of Byzantine history, gunpowder began to be used throughout Europe for military purposes. The empire did use some heavy guns but not as extensively as the Ottoman Turks. The fall of Constantinople in 1453 AD was mainly due to the guns of the Ottoman army, against which the city's defenders had nothing of comparable firepower. The limited use of artillery was an immediate consequence of the economic weakness of the Byzantine state. The first guns used by the Byzantine army were intermediate size bombards, 1 meter long with a caliber of 20 cm. It also appears that the Byzantine army continued using Greek fire, the formula of which remained the most strictly guarded secret until the final collapse of the empire. Some eastern armies had begun to use variants of Greek fire that was, however, less effective.

The campaigning season was usually from March until the autumn, although at times this was extended until December. During a campaign, the army's nucleus was the mercenaries and the *pronoiars*. The latter did not participate when a campaign was hurriedly organized, as it was not possible for them to be rapidly assembled. Aside from these forces, the army also included a host of servants and auxiliary personnel, along with different types of lightly armed soldiers, usually gathered from the rural population and the city's poor. The lightly armed soldiers were actually an auxiliary force, which would not play any decisive role during the course of the campaign. Indeed, their participation was so limited that it was often considered unimportant. They mobilized in the hope of

Fortified tower at the Chilandari Monastery, Mt. Athos.

The tower of the castle at Platamon.

gaining some profit from the spoils of the war or in the belief that they were fighting for a just cause or for their homeland. The Byzantine armies of that time, consisting of unruly, disorganized groups of mercenaries, indifferent *pronoiars* and a horde of ragamuffin, lightly armed soldiers or auxiliary personnel and servants, looked rather like roving hordes or ill-disciplined mobs. They were, in no way, reminiscent of the disciplined, well-organized forces that Belisarius or Basil II the Boulgaroktonos had led into battle.

On campaign, small groups of skirmishers, called *koursatores,* always ranged ahead of the invading army. Their mission was to cause confusion in the enemy's regions, by raiding as well as assembling quantities of supplies and as much loot as possible, in order to raise the army's morale. In many instances, the undisciplined armies of that time resorted to plunder without the approval of their commanders, who were forced to tolerate the behavior of their troops. In most cases, however, the senior officers did not even know the exact number of the men under their command, as numbers of soldiers would desert while others would join depending on the place, duration of the campaign and the development of the military operations. The endemic indiscipline caused frequent conflicts among the men that were solved by the army's arbiter, a dignitary between a provost and a negotiator for the resolution of problems caused by offences or by conflicts arising from the distribution of loot. During the course of the campaign, the army halted at camps, which obviously bore no relation to the organized camps set up by the legions of late antiquity or the Byzantine armies of the middle period. The security of the camp was a duty undertaken by the *Megas Domestikos tis Viglas*, who, despite his impressive title, was a junior officer whose job was to co-ordinate the guard *(imeroviglion)*, that usually consisted of lightly armed archers. When the camp was near the enemy, various stratagems were carried out in order to deceive them. Prior to the Battle of Pelagonia in 1259 AD, the *Megas Domestikos*, John Palaiologos, ordered the local villagers to light many fires each evening, to give the impression that a large army was bivouacked in the area, and to cross the adjacent hillsides on their mules and donkeys, to give the appearance of powerful cavalry forces on the move.

The fortifications and their importance

During the turbulent late period of the Byzantine saga, the possession of fortified sites was of particular importance. The role of these fortresses was multiple. The local governors' headquarters were situated in them and it was only there that any economic activity could develop in safety. They also stood guard over the imperial family's treasures and those of the aristocracy and, in addition, the inhabitants of the countryside took refuge in them in times of civil unrest or hostile raids. The fortified settlements were called *kastra* ("castles," from the Latin term *castrum*). The formal *kastron* consisted of a fortified hill, on which a strong citadel was built. The sides of the hill were also fortified, providing protection for all the adjacent settlement or at least a part of it. The two main social classes had separate facilities in the castle. Commoners stayed in a different area from the upper classes' residences, affording protection to the nobles from any disturbances that might erupt among the poor.

In cases of absolute necessity, when the rest of the settlement had been occupied, the citadel could be used as the ultimate bunker and last line of defense. To maintain and improve the fortifications was a special task, called *kastroktisia*, for the population, however, the majority of monasteries and the villeins who cultivated their land, were exempted from this obligation.

Apart from the castles that were, in fact, fortified settlements, there were also other fortresses, such as the independent towers that were built to maintain control over places of strategic importance or used as treasuries and bunkers for the powerful country families and their villeins. The Tower of Pythion on the Evros river, built in the middle of the 14th century by John VI Kantakouzenos, is a prime example. The monasteries were also fortified with high precincts and strong towers, so that, externally, they differed little from the towers of the aristocracy in the countryside. The greatest fortification work of the late period was *Examilion*, the wall that Manuel II Palaiologos built in 1415 AD – 1416 AD at the Corinth Isthmus in order to prevent the Turkish invasions of the Peloponnesus. It was a significant project, almost equal to the walls of Constantinople. The wall covered the whole width of Isthmus and had 153 towers, moats and two strong fortresses at its two ends, one on the Gulf of Corinth and the other on the Gulf of Saronikos. Another special tax, called *floriatikon*, was imposed on residents of that region to maintain the *Examilion* and for the recruitment of mercenaries to protect the Byzantine possessions of the

The tower of Pythion at Ebros was an important base for John VI Kantakouzenos.

Peloponnesus. The *Examilion*, however, did not protect the Peloponnesus from the Turkish raids. The Turks destroyed it in 1423 AD. The Byzantines rebuilt it in 1443 AD but the Ottomans destroyed it yet again three years later, in 1446 AD; part of it, however, existed until 1452 AD, and it was with great difficulty that the Turks, who attacked the Peloponnesus, managed to pass through the *Examilion*. During the 17th century, the Venetians, who temporarily possessed the Peloponnesus, discovered the remains of the wall and tried to rebuild it, although without success. Ruins of the fortifications still exist in a number of places.

The castles' garrisons consisted of two categories of men, regular troops and members of the local militia. A guard of regular soldiers usually existed only in the most important castles. In the remainder of them, there was only a small force under the command of the local governor. In the event of hostilities, this force could be strengthened with mercenaries and militia. If the settlement came under attack, all the inhabitants would participate in its defense, not only the members of the militia. Often this assistance proved critical, as the garrison contingent was usually small and was not strong enough to resist any attacker alone. The castle garrison usually consisted of 250 to 400 soldiers although it could, however, be much smaller. When the Turks occupied the Pringiponisia (Prince's Island) near Constantinople in 1453 AD, the garrison consisted of a mere 30 men.

There were a number of cases, however, where the local population coerced the garrison into undertaking risky actions. In 1342 AD, a Mongol band reached Skopelos in Thrace. The governor of the city, realizing that the garrison under his command was too weak to resist them, preferred not to face them in open battle but, instead, kept his forces within the city walls, sure that the feckless Mongols would withdraw once they had completed plundering the surrounding countryside. The city's inhabitants, however, reacting to the sight of the destruction wreaked by the invaders on their fields, demanded that the garrison venture out from the city and drive off the Mongols. The governor refused, with the result that the residents arrested him and locked him up in the castle prison. The members of the guard, meanwhile, decided to cooperate with the inhabitants and finally attacked the Mongols, but with disastrous results. They were routed, with the only survivors of the battle being a few horsemen who managed to escape at full gallop.

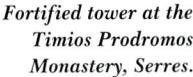

Fortified tower at the Timios Prodromos Monastery, Serres.

Conclusion

Throughout the entire life span of the empire, a large part of the forces that defended it consisted of foreign mercenaries. This practice led to the Byzantine state depending on groups of adventurers, the reliability of whom was proportionate to their salary. Internal forces of the empire, unfortunately, undermined the native soldier/farmer class that constituted an alternative solution to the need to recruit mercenaries. The most important factors leading to the weakening of the army and the empire's defenses was the shortsighted bureaucracy that, at times, surrounded the imperial administration, and the major landowners who were insatiable in their constant greed for land and power. These groups brought about the final collapse, as they eagerly defended their narrow interests against the soldier/farmers, without taking into consideration the fact that the survival of the empire depended on the effectiveness of the Byzantine army. Despite these fundamental problems in the social and political structure of the empire, however, it cannot be denied that the Byzantine army successfully fulfilled its mission for many long centuries. The Middle Ages was a period of hostility and ostentation. Securing the survival of the Byzantine Empire for eleven centuries in such a hostile environment, threatened by so many powerful enemies, was undeniably a major achievement. This success is owed to the resolve and the bravery of the soldiers of the Byzantine state, regardless of their origin and the motives for which they served in the army.

The tower of a Byzantine fortress in the area of Macedonia, northern Greece.

Bibliography

The author gratefully acknowledges the following sources:

Bartusis, Mark C., *The Late Byzantine Army: arms and society, 1204-1453*, Philadelphia, University of Pennsylvania Press, 1992.

Baynes, Norman H. and Moss, H.St.L.B., *Byzantium, an Introduction to East Roman Civilisation*, Oxford, Clarendon Press, 1961.

Haldon, John, *Warfare, State and Society in the Byzantine world 565 - 1204*, London, UCL Press, 1999.

Haldon, John, *The Byzantine Wars,* Stroud, Tempus Publishing Group, 2001.

Heath, Ian, *Byzantine Armies 886 - 1118*, London, Osprey, 1981.

Kean, Roger Michael, *Forgotten Power: Byzantium: Bulwark of Christianity,* Ludlow: Thalamus Publishing, 2005.

Kolias, Taxiarchis G., *Byzantinische Waffen: ein Beitrag zur byzantinischen Waffenkunde von den Anfängen bis zur lateinischen Eroberung,* Wien, Österreichische Akademie der Wissenschaften, 1988.

Leo VI, Emperor of the East, 866 - 912, *Tactica,* (English and Greek text, pp. 1004-1073, bound with Volume 2 of Polyaenus, *Strategems of War*), Chicago, Ares Press, 1994.

Nicolle, David, *Romano-Byzantine Armies 4th - 9th Centuries*, London, Osprey, 1992.

Ostrogorsky, Georgije, *Geschichte des byzantinischen Staates,* München, C. H. Beck, 1952.

Ostrogorsky, Georgije, *History of the Byzantine State,* (Joan Hussey, trans.) Oxford, Blackwell, 1980.

Ravegnani, Giorgio, *I Byzantini e la guerra*, Roma, Jouvence, 2004.

Runciman, Steven, *A History of the Crusades*, Cambridge, Cambridge University Press, 1954.

Southern, Pat & Dixon, Karen R., *The Late Roman Army*, London, Routledge, 2000.

Turnbull, Stephen, *The Walls of Constantinople AD 324 - 1453*, Oxford, Osprey Publishing, 2004.

Christophilopoulou, Aikaterina, *Byzantine History,* (W.W. Phelps, trans.) Amsterdam, A.M. Hakkert, 1993.

Glossary

Greek terms

Akrites: local military aristocracy, living along the empire's borders protecting them from Arab raids. They built their own fortresses and maintained a relative autonomy from the central administration in Constantinople. As a legend, they became part of modern Greek tradition.

Allaghion: during the middle period it was a military unit consisting of four *lochagiai*. During the late period, it simply constituted a large group of soldiers, being the basic part of a subdivision of an army.

Apelatikion: mace, club augmented by three, four or six spikes.

Archegetes: rank corresponding to the *hoplitarches* or the leader of all military forces.

Athanatoi (the "Immortals"): elite unit of the emperor's bodyguard during the reign of Alexios I Komnenos.

Bandon: martial emblem of a unit or a military unit under the administration of a count, consisting of approximately 200 soldiers.

Bandophoros or "bandoforus" or "draconarius": elite soldier whose primary duty was to carry his unit's emblem, a standard-bearer.

Chartoularata: government owned stud for horses in the Balkan provinces.

Chartoularios: dignitary administrating a "theme," responsible for the central administration's taxation and other state incomes.

Cheirosiphon: a portable device, which could be carried by a single soldier, for launching Greek fire.

Chortasmata: forage that the members of the cavalry units received for their animals.

Chonsarioi: groups of mercenaries who carried out raids in the empire's hostile Balkan border territory.

Domestikos: highest military rank. A Domesticos administered each one of the four units of the tagmata, except for the numerus, the commander of which was a droungarios. Superior among these was the "Domesticos of the Scholae." Later, this rank and the corresponding administration was divided: there was a "Domesticos of the Scholae of the East" (for the Asiatic provinces) and a "Domesticos of the Scholae of the West" (for the European provinces).

Domestikos tis viglas: holder of a low rank, in charge of coordinating the guard (*imeroviglion*).

Dorea ("donation"): special donation to soldiers on the occasion of certain anniversaries or exceptional events, such as the appointment of a new emperor. It was the continuation of the Roman *donativum*.

Doryphoroi or "hypaspistai": mercenaries who served in the personal units of various generals as *Bucellarii*.

Droungarios: commander of a *droungos*.

Droungos or "moira": military unit, subdivision of a *tourma*. It fell under the command of either a *droungarios* or a *moirarches*.

Droungarokomes: the rank after the ranks of the *droungarios* and the *komes* were united.

Druzhina: unit of 6,000 mercenaries sent to Constantinople in 988 AD by the sovereign Vladimir of Kiev to serve Emperor Basil II, the Boulgaroktonos, (976 AD – 1025 AD). It was this unit that constituted the basis of the Varangian guard.

Doucatores: special officers in charge of planning the details of a march.

Dynatoi: powerful landowners, who tried to extend their power by undermining central imperial power. They had acquired large tracts of land, much wealth and, in many cases they had fortified their mansions and hired groups of mercenaries.

Epilorikion: thick tunic, worn over the breastplate.

Ethnarches: title of dignitaries who administered units of foreign mercenaries (*ethni*, meaning "nations").

Examilion: wall built at Isthmus to prevent the Turkish incursions in the Peloponnesus.

Excubitoi ("excubitors," meaning "Watchmen"):

elite unit of the emperor's bodyguard during the reign of Alexios I Komnenos.

Flamouliskia: metal pieces for shoulder protection, embellished with small colorful strips to impress the enemy.

Flamoulon: small pennant affixed just below the head of a cavalryman's lance.

Greek fire: in Greek *hygron pyr*, meaning "liquid fire," flammable mixture, the composition of which was one of the empire's most closely guarded secrets.

Hikanatoi (the "Worthy"): unit of the emperor's guard and part of the *tagmata*.

Hoplitarches: officer superior to the *taxiarches*, commander of a large unit, consisting primarily of infantry.

Ilarchos: lieutenant governor of a *bandon* of cavalry.

Kabadion or "bambakion": tunic worn by the soldiers under their breastplates, primarily to cushion any blow by the enemy. This was used by the infantry more often than by the cavalry.

Kastroktisia: fiscal charge in the form of corvé labor (a day's unpaid labor) imposed on the populace for the maintenance and improvement of fortifications.

Kastron: castle, fortified settlement. The typical "castle" consisted of a fortified hill, on which was constructed a powerful citadel. The hillsides were also fortified and might include part of an adjacent settlement.

Kataphraktoi ("cataphracts"): heavily armed horsemen.

Kefalai (the "Heads"): provincial governors.

Kentarchos: centurion.

Kleisourarchiai: special areas for the security of points of strategic importance along the frontiers.

Klibanion: type of body armor.

Kontaratoi: soldiers armed with spears.

Korys or "kassis:" type of helmet.

Koursatores ("skirmishers"): small groups of raiders, who advanced ahead of the army during a campaign.

Krites tou foussatou (the "Arbiter of the Army"): negotiator to resolve problems caused by offences or disputes arising from the distribution of captured loot.

Lochagia: subdivision of a *bandon*, under the administration of a *lochagos* ("captain").

Lorikion: type of breastplate. The word comes from the Latin term *lorica*.

Martzobaboulon: small lead javelin.

Mensouratores: survey officers in charge of troop encampments.

Merarchos or "stratelate": the military governor of a *meros*, division commander

Meros or "tourma": military unit consisting of three *moirai* with a divisional commander or *stratelates* in command. It consisted of 3,000 troops, but this number could be increased to 6,000 or even 7,000 men.

Moira or "droungos": unit superior to the *numerus*, initially under the command of a *Dux*, but later of a *Droungarios* or *Moirarches*. The numerical force of a *moira* never exceeded 3,000 men.

"Moirarches" or "chiliarches": the military governor of a *moira* or *droungos*.

Ouragos: the "Rear officer," file closer, a junior officer rank.

Paramerion: single-edged sabre.

Parataxis: cavalry unit consisting of 10 *banda* of 50 horsemen each.

Parateichion: open space 20 meters wide between the moat and the first wall of Constantinople.

Paximadion or "paximation": Greek name for the Roman army's hardtack (*bucella* or *bucellatum*) rations.

Pentekontarchiai: *allaghia* consisting of 50 horsemen, which, at the close of the 9th century, replaced the cavalry "centuries."

Praetor: dignitary administering a "theme," person responsible for the application of law and the control of services.

Peribolos: precinct, the space between Constantinople's interior and exterior wall.

Pronoia: the grant of state revenue usually in return for military service.

Pronoiars: those who had been granted a *pronoia*.

Protonotarios: dignitary responsible for the economic management of a "theme," liable to the *genikon logothesion* (one of the ministries of the empire), checking the logistics, the soldiers' salaries, concentrating the necessary supplies when, in case of a campaign, the imperial army crossed his jurisdiction.

Protostrator: during the 9th century he was

the military governor of the emperor's mounted entourage. During the 11th century, the *protostratores* emerged as lieutenant governors of the imperial armies, immediately subordinate to the *Domesticoi* of the East and the West in the hierarchy of the imperial army.

Scholae ("scholae palatinae"): name of the emperor's personal guard.

Scholarioi or "scholares": soldiers serving in the *scholae*.

Scorpions: stone-throwing catapults.

Scutatoi: spearmen serving in the units of heavy infantry.

Sticharion: in Latin *sticharium*, the legionaries' robe.

Strateia: the obligation weighing on the farmer/soldiers.

Stratos: army, a force of various military units, consisting of three parts, with a general *(Strategos)* as military governor. A small army usually consisting of 5,000 soldiers, a medium one from 5,000 to 15,000 men, and a large one could be between 20,000 men or 24,000 men, if also accompanied by cavalry units.

Syndosis: collaboration by a number of property holders, who were responsible for military service, to pool the expenses for the upkeep of a soldier.

Syntrophiai: means companies, Byzantine name for mercenary companies.

Tagmata: military force primarily consisting of more flexible units of mercenaries that were initially stationed in the capital, but later stationed in all the major cities. At their core was the emperor's bodyguard.

Taxiarches: military governor of a brigade.

Taxiarchia: military unit corresponding in force to a *chiliarchia*, consisting of 500 spearmen, 200 *kontaratoi* (soldiers armed with lances) and 300 archers.

Themata ("themes"): military and political administrative areas. The term was initially identified with military units under the administration of a general. Later, the same term was also attributed to the region where those units were stationed.

Touldon or "touldos": convoy transporting the supplies of the entire army (siege engines, foodstuffs and weapons).

Trapezitai or "trasinarioi": small groups of elite soldiers with the basic mission of conducting raids into hostile territory along the empire's eastern borders.

"Tourma" or "meros": military unit, subdivision of a "theme."

Tourmarches or "merarchos": military governor of a *tourma*. There were two categories, the superior *(prokritoteroi)* and the junior ones *(elattoteroi)*.

Triboloi: small metal spikes. Each *tribolos* had four spikes and was manufactured so that, if thrown on the ground, a spike always stood upright. In this way, the *triboloi* acted as a means of delaying or hindering the movement of enemy soldiers and/or animals.

Varangians: the most famous unit of the emperor's bodyguard. It was created during the reign of Basil II, the Boulgaroktonos. The members of the guard were, initially, from Scandinavia, but later were almost exclusively Saxons from England. A number of reports of the continued survival of the Varangian guard existed until the beginning of the 15th century.

Vigliatikon: tax imposed for military purposes.

Zabai: type of breastplate.

Latin terms

Adgestum ("pile"): mound that was constructed equal to, or higher than the walls of a besieged fortress and forming the base for the ballistic machines.

Agmen: *moira*, unit of the Roman – Byzantine army.

Agri Limitanei: fields along the borders, cultivable plots of land for maintaining the soldiers guarding the borders.

Alae (in Latin, "Pteryges" in Greek, meaning "wings"): auxiliary units of the Roman army made up exclusively of horsemen.

Annona: amount of money that was equal to the basic salary that every soldier earned.

Annona Foederatica: supplies provided to the *Foederati* for their maintenance.

Aries (in Latin, "Krios" in Greek, meaning "ram"): a large movable shed, equipped with wheels, constructed of timber and protected on the outside by skins. The interior contained a large girder, a battering ram with a sharpened point, strengthened with metal usually in form of an obelisk or, less often, four-squared. The girder could move freely to and fro and was used to continuously strike at a given point of the walls. During Justinian's reign, a lighter design of battering ram was devised, without wheels, which could be transported on the backs of 40 men.

Aurem tironicum: redemption gold, pecuniary sum, the payment of which replaced the obligation of enlistment.

Auxilia: units of light auxiliary cavalry in Constantine the Great's army.

Ballistae: catapults for launching arrows or rocks.

Ballistarii: soldiers who handled the stone-throwing catapults *(ballistae)*.

Biarchus: junior officer who undertook the duties of a quartermaster.

Bucella or "bucellatum": the Roman army's hardtack rations, called paximadion or *paximation* in Greek.

Bucellarii: the term comes from the word *bucella* or *bucellatum* (Roman army hardtack). It initially characterized the mercenaries who worked for the major landowners and protected their properties and mansions from the ravages of other barbarians or rapacious gangs. Progressively, however, the term *Bucellarii* also became the term used for some of the imperial army's mercenaries, specifically those that had been recruited after an agreement with a particular general but not with the emperor.

Burgi: small fortified places, including fortified stations or small independent towers.

Candidati ("white-robed"): military unit consisting of 40 elite *palatini*.

Capitatio: type of head tax from which the veteran legionaries were exempt.

Capitus: quantity of forage that was given to the cavalrymen for the maintenance of their horses.

Causaria missio: justifiable discharge from military service awarded to Legionaries due to wounds received in battle or for other health reasons.

Centurio or "centenaries": centurion.

Cohortes peditae: units of Roman army infantry.

Cohortes equitae: units of the Roman army, consisting mainly of horsemen.

Comitatenses: soldiers of the Roman army serving in more flexible units in the empire's rear areas, and not for maintaining border security.

Comes: military governor of a *numerus* or an even larger military unit.

Comes excubitorum: military governor of a unit of the *Excubitors*.

Comites limitis: dignitaries responsible for the security of the border regions.

Comites rei miltaris: military dignitaries, whose area of responsibility could cover an insignificant frontier station or the governance of an entire province. Usually, however, this title was identified by the rank of *Dux*.

Contus: long lance of the cavalry units.

Cunei equitum: auxiliary units of cavalry in Constantine's army.

Decurio: in Greek *dekarchos*, military commander of a small group of ten soldiers.

Defensores: spearmen who carried out defensive missions.

Donativum: the sum that a legionary saved from the donations given by the emperors. In the Byzantine army, this institution continued under the name *dorea (donation)*.

Draco: a unit's military standard, which often took the form of a dragon.

Draconarius: junior officer, standard-bearer, who carried a unit's standard *(draco)*.

Ducenarius: military commander of a unit of 200 soldiers.

Duces or "duces limitis": military governors of units of *Ripenses* that were stationed along the frontier provinces.

Dux Aegypti: military governor of Egypt.

Dux Africae: military governor of the Roman provinces of Northwest Africa.

Emerita missio: "meritorious discharge" i.e., well-earned retirement pay, awarded to soldiers following a long service career, usually 24 years.

Equites: the horsemen of the Roman army.

Fabricae: state factories for armament production. The most usual fabricae were those that manufactured shields and other types of basic armament (fabricae scutariae et armorum), but there were also "fabricae" that manufactured bows and arrows *(fabricae sagittariae et arquariae)*.

Fabricenses: those who worked in the state factories for armament production.

Foederati: barbarian mercenaries serving the empire.

Foedus: the agreement between the barbarian mercenaries and the emperor.

Hasta plumbata: type of javelin of which there were two types, *hasta plumbata et tribolata* and *hasta plumbata mamillata*. The *plumbata et tribolata* had the form of a sharp cylinder (with a handgrip of metal or wood). The handgrip at the lower end had small feathers attached to it to steady it when thrown. The *plumbata mamillata* had a lead weight behind the metal point and feathers at the opposite end of the handgrip.

Honesta missio: honorable discharge and retirement pay, awarded to soldiers who had completed military service of, at least, 20 years.

Horrea: state-owned fortified supply depots under the protection of the army.

Hospes: guest soldier; the term was applied to a soldier who was given lodging in the residence of a citizen of the empire.

Limes: the line of the Roman frontier.

Limitanei: "ripenses," the soldiers that guarded the Roman Empire's borders.

Loca or "territoria castellorum": cultivable plots of land around a castle to provide food for the soldiers guarding the borders.

Lorica hamata: breastplate constructed of metal rings.

Lorica squamata: breastplate constructed of small metal plates, connected by strips of leather or linen cloth.

Lupi ("wolves"): wooden planks through which a number of nails had been hammered so the points protruded. The nails were also called "the wolves teeth," which gave this piece of military hardware its name. The planks were supported on two stakes and then placed above the gates. When an enemy approached to launch an attack, the "wolves" were allowed to fall on the assailants, causing many casualties.

Magister equitum ("magister of the cavalrymen"): military commander of all units of cavalry of the Roman army.

Magister in praesenti or "magister praesentalis": the *magister peditum* or *equitum* was stationed at the Imperial court under the direct supervision of the emperor. In the Western Roman Empire, the magister *peditum praesentalis* was responsible for the general administration of the entire army.

Magister Militum: the military governor of each one of the important units of the *Comitatenses* stationed in Gaul, Illyria (current north-western Balkans), Thrace (this province included the entire north-eastern part of the Balkans) and the empire's eastern borders.

Magister Militum per Armeniam: military governor of the forces along the empire's eastern borders. This rank was created in 528 AD after the division of the jurisdictional region of the *Magister Militum per Orientem*. The *Magister Militum per Armeniam* was stationed in Theodosioupoli (modern Erzurum of Turkey) and his area of jurisdiction covered the empire's eastern borders from the Black Sea coasts to Martyropoli (modern Silban of Turkey), east of Amida (modern Diyarbakir of Turkey).

Magister Militum per Gallias: military governor of the *Comitatenses* stationed in Gaul.

Magister Militum per Illyricum: military governor of the *Comitatenses* stationed in Illyria (current north-western Balkans).

Magister Militum per Orientem: military governor of the *Comitatenses* stationed along the empire's eastern borders.

Magister Militum per Thracias: military governor of the *Comitatenses* stationed in Thrace (this province included all the north-eastern area of the Balkans).

Magister peditum ("magister of the infantrymen"): military governor of all units of infantry in the Roman army.

Magister officiorum: dignitary responsible for the control of the economic management of the *scholae*.

Maiordomus: the chief-of-staff of dignitaries' entire personnel, also including the *Bucellarii*.

Mansiones: guest houses along the Roman roads, where dignitaries, soldiers and postmen could stay overnight.

Milliaria: units of the Roman army amounting to 1,000 men.

Milites castellani or "castresiani": soldiers manning the frontier fortresses.

Numerarii: junior officers dealing with economic questions.

Numerus: "number," basic military unit. One complete numerus consisted of 500 soldiers, but often the term was also attributed to units of a larger or smaller force. In reality, each numerus consisted of 200 to 400 soldiers, most usually around 300.

Officium: the staff of a *Magister Militum*.

Officiales: the officers that served on the staff of a *Magister Militum* or *Dux*.

Optio: employee responsible for the payment of a dignitary's entire staff, also including the *Bucellarii*.

Palatini: name given to soldiers serving in the units of the *Comitatenses* to distinguish them from those serving on the borders.

Pallium: the legionary's cloak.

Pedites: the Roman army's infantry.

Pilum: the Roman army's classic javelin.

Praefectus praetorio ("custodian of the Praetorium"): initially he was the military governor of the praetorian guard; after Constantine the Great's military reforms, however, the term was changed to encompass the person responsible for the army's catering and supplies.

Praepositus: the term initially applied to the commander of a military unit while it was being relocated. Afterwards, the title was attributed to governors of smaller units. Depending on the unit in which they served, they were distinguished as *praepositi scholae* if they belonged to the emperor's bodyguard, praepositi legionis if they belonged to a particular legion, or *praepositi cohortis* if they administered particular smaller units of legionaries. There also existed a *praepositi equitum* for the cavalry; *praepositi auxilii* for the auxiliary units of barbarian mercenaries and, in certain cases, there was also a more general term of *praepositi militum*. Along the borders there also existed smaller administrations, each one coming under a *praepositus limitis*.

Praepositus castri: commander of a fortress.

Praeses: the political governor of a Roman province.

Primicerius: the highest rank of the junior officers in Constantine's army.

Principia: administration offices in the Roman fortresses.

Probatio: trial period for newly recruited legionaries, before they were officially accepted onto the strength of their unit.

Protectores (protectors): unit of the emperor's guard, the soldiers of which were divided into *protectores* and *protectores domestici*. The *protectores domestici* were considered superior and were

named *praesentales*, if they served in Constantinople, or *deputati*, if they served elsewhere. The *protectores* were separated into units that were also called *scholae* and consisted of units of infantry or cavalry. The military governors of these units were called *primicerii*. The protectores *domestici praesentales* numbered roughly 200 men, the precise number of the remainder being unknown. In the past, the simple *protectores* constituted a fighting unit of the emperor's guard. During Justinian's time, however, they had lost their battle readiness and dealt exclusively with court duties.

Pugio: type of dagger of the Roman army.

Quadriburgium: square fortress with a tower at each corner.

Quingenaria: units of the Roman army amounting to 500 men.

Refugia: shelters, fortresses along the Roman borders, where the Roman army could take refuge in case of barbarian raids.

Ripenses: *Limitanei*, the soldiers that protected the borders of the Roman Empire.

Sacramentum: the legionnaire's military oath.

Sagitarii: archers.

Scholae palatinae: units of the emperor's guard.

Scribones: armed unit of the emperor's guard. It is unknown if they constituted a separate unit of the emperor's bodyguard or simply the officer cadre of the *Excubitors*. Often they were used for important and/or dangerous missions.

Senator: junior rank in the infantry and *scholae* units.

Signaculum: small lead disk, which the legionaries hung round their necks.

Stipendium: a legionary's salary.

Testudina (in Latin; in Greek "Chelones," meaning "turtles"): shelters under which soldiers could take cover in order to advance on the walls of a city or fortress to which they were laying siege.

Tribunus: military commander of a *numerus*.

Vicarious: lieutenant governor of a *Magister Militum*.

Vinea: the word in Latin means "climbing vine" or "gallery." The vinea was a movable shed under which besiegers could safely move round the walls of the city or fortress to which they were laying siege.